# Discoveries by

## Tropical Living

## Spout and About

At Frederick P. Victoria & Son (212-813-9651; www.fpvictoria.com), a graceful watering can, circa 1955, fashioned of brass and copper from Austria's Hagenauer Workshops, $1,200, was discovered.

## Lo

An 1
*luoh*
Park
Furn
of la
of "V

# Tropical Living

## Contemporary Dream Houses in the Philippines

by Elizabeth V. Reyes

with Fernando Nakpil Zialcita and Paulo Alcazaren

photography by Chester Ong

PERIPLUS

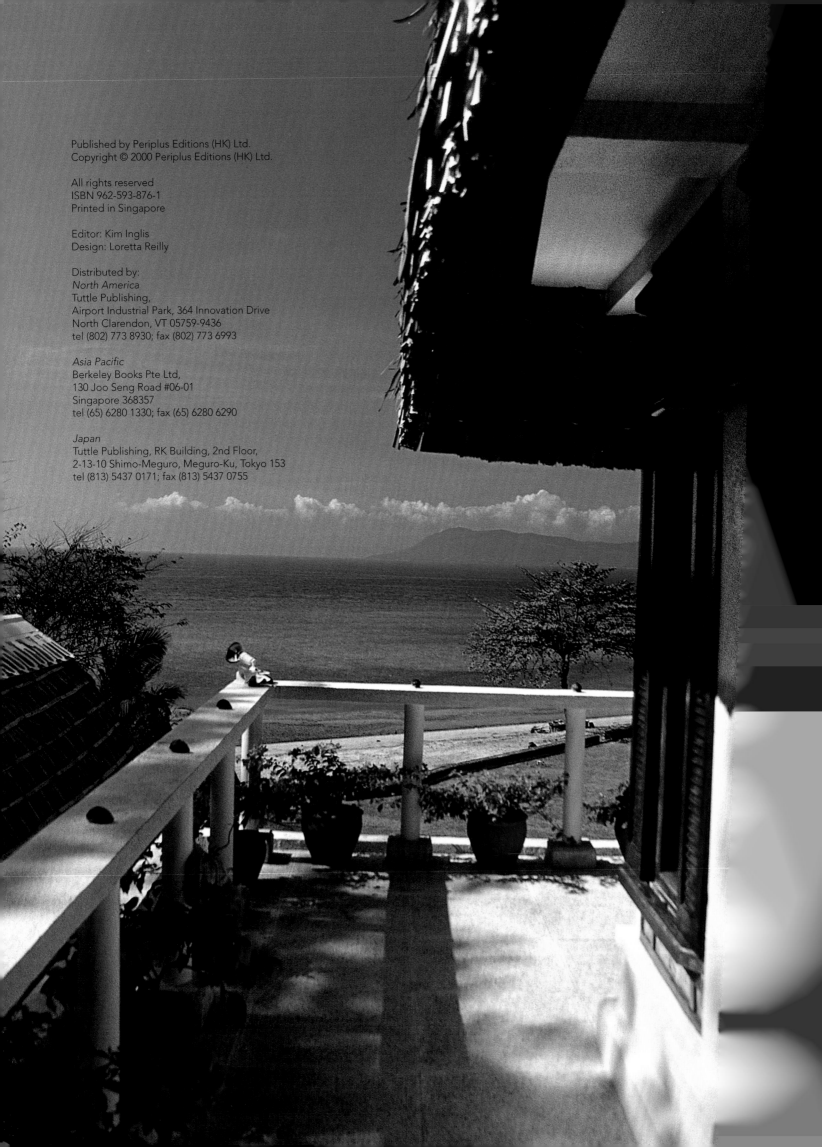

Published by Periplus Editions (HK) Ltd.
Copyright © 2000 Periplus Editions (HK) Ltd.

All rights reserved
ISBN 962-593-876-1
Printed in Singapore

Editor: Kim Inglis
Design: Loretta Reilly

Distributed by:
*North America*
Tuttle Publishing,
Airport Industrial Park, 364 Innovation Drive
North Clarendon, VT 05759-9436
tel (802) 773 8930; fax (802) 773 6993

*Asia Pacific*
Berkeley Books Pte Ltd,
130 Joo Seng Road #06-01
Singapore 368357
tel (65) 6280 1330; fax (65) 6280 6290

*Japan*
Tuttle Publishing, RK Building, 2nd Floor,
2-13-10 Shimo-Meguro, Meguro-Ku, Tokyo 153
tel (813) 5437 0171; fax (813) 5437 0755

# contents

# a different tropical style

The Republic of the Philippines shares with Indonesia the distinction of being the largest tropical archipelagos in the world. It has 7,100 islands, which range from small coral atolls to huge islands with deep forests and towering volcanoes. Wherever one travels in this beguiling land, there is always the promise of a breezy tropical scene; and there is always a new beach, with swaying palm trees and clear blue skies, where warm waves break and slide over the sands.

In tune with the country and climate is a relaxed, contemporary architectural style. Homes are tropical, exotic, romantic; there is a prodigious use of light and space; breezes flow through rooms, cooling and caressing occupants. A permanent feature is the *lanai*, a type of verandah that has wide eaves to shelter the interior from the sun and is open to the elements on at least three sides, thus ensuring the free flow of cooling breezes. In many cases it acts as an alternative to the more formal dining room. It is the place to lounge in, to relax in, to take in the scents of a tropical garden.

Filipino house design also reflects other features of the environment, such as the sea or the forests. For centuries, the *capiz* shell, a bivalve flatter than the oyster and more translucent when cleaned, has been used as the tiny panes of traditional wooden grid-windows. In modern design, *capiz* shell finds new applications, such as in lightboxes, picture frames or as tear drops in chandeliers. Furthermore, people who can afford it furnish their houses with increasingly rare local hardwoods which are superior in density and texture; one such example is the *narra*, a fragrant wood with an intense sienna color.

In recent decades, other woods from the foothills are being used. Examples include coconut and bamboo trunks which, when split, flattened, diced, and laminated, are transformed into classy boards with unexpected textures.

There are many varieties of house design in the Philippines. Consider the *lanai*. One common interpretation used in beach houses is a simple structure of bent wooden columns that draw the thatch roof and split-bamboo ceiling close to the ground. Just as popular is the Mediterranean variation: eaves of curved red tiles, plain stone pillars, and tiled floors. Or the starkly simple: a cantilevered concrete roof and highly polished marble floor that together extend outward to meet the sky and the lawn. There are also the personal, one-of-a-kind interpretations, such as the *lanai* that marries stone columns with ornate capitals and lace-like metal tracery on the roof edge.

Variety likewise characterizes Filipino furniture. Bauhaus inspires the locally made, severely simple furniture in stainless steel, vinyl and glass; or, lately, comfortable sofas that combine wood and *abaca*, an extremely versatile hemp fiber. Yet other furniture styles include Mediterranean-inspired designs with a lavish use of scrolls and iron as the predominant material. Others draw on influences closer to home and simplify the horseshoe-shaped back- and arm-rests and curving back slats of Chinese chairs. There are, of course, other designs that cannot be readily pigeon-holed. One example is designer Ernest Santiago's highly personal and comfortable long chair that evokes a river bank. Formed from multiple materials—twisted driftwood for the

backrest, river stones for support, and flat serrated driftwood for the seat, it is a highly individualistic piece.

Unfortunately, Filipino design is little known abroad. Despite the extensive use of English in the country, the Philippines seems to have received less publicity than its neighbors. But in an era that increasingly appreciates cultural fusions between East and West, the Philippines is set to play a unique role as one of the original fusion cultures. Filipinos belong to the Austronesian-speaking peoples who populated an island realm that extended from Madagascar to Southeast Asia to Polynesia. Their indigenous houses were frame constructions with raised floors, built near or over water. Thatched roofs were steeply pitched to facilitate the release of hot tropical air and to drain off heavy rain. Wooden columns dug deep into the ground supported the trusses (these columns sway during the frequent earthquakes). Timber or bamboo walls were merely screens to keep out sun and wind. Furnishings were sparse: a low table, chests, and, in the absence of beds and chairs, woven straw mats.

In the late 16th century, Spanish colonial influence introduced stone and tile. However, earthquake conditions compelled builders to develop a "mixed style" (*arquitectura mestiza*), where solid wooden pillars of native tradition were implanted in curtain walls of stone or brick, thus defining room spaces. The upper-story walls of these new Filipino houses were made of wood and had large window openings with sliding panels of translucent *capiz* shell panes in checkerboard pattern. They recalled Japanese *shoji* screens, for along with the Chinese came Japanese settlers. The wood-and-stone Filipino house marries continents.

Other influences are evident. Seventeenth-century Manila was the anchor of the galleon trade, the first global commercial network to link three continents. Island-made galleons brought precious Oriental goods to Mexico, which then shipped them on to the Americas and Europe. In exchange, highly prized Mexican silver entered the Orient and enabled Filipinos to construct grand houses that bridged East and West. Tables, chairs, and commodes, inspired by European styles but in island hardwood, appeared. Décor was eclectic: saints carved from Indian ivories, Chinese lacquered screens, and Persian carpets, for example, may have been displayed in one room.

Modern building technology appeared in the twilight years of Spanish rule and became widespread after the U.S. took over in 1898. Public buildings, offices, and residences built in reinforced concrete in modernist styles, from Art Deco to the International, appeared. Although many buildings were destroyed during the Japanese Occupation of 1942–1945, after 1946 reconstruction following independence encouraged experimentation with modernist styles. Schools teaching contemporary design opened.

Some observations can be made about modernism in the Philippines. First, the partnership between the ubiquitous thatch and bent wooden columns continues to inspire architects who love the seemingly "natural." Second, the presence of both massive stonework (in the ground floor) and light woodwork (in the upper story) illustrates the way in which Filipino architects are attracted to experimentation with voluminous shapes as well as lean, linear forms. Third, the fact that the houses bring stylistic traditions together encourages Filipinos today to explore different architectural traditions. They feel equally at home with the stucco arches of the Mediterranean, as they do among the steeply-pitched hipped roofs, wide eaves, lavish woodwork, and translucent windows of East Asia. A discriminating cosmopolitanism characterizes the best of today's Filipino design.

One major stream of "modern" architecture, the so-called "Prairie Style" of Frank Lloyd Wright, acclimatizes well because there are many parallels with local traditions. The Prairie Style integrates a building with its landscape. Horizontal planes and organic-looking materials—such as irregularly shaped stones and wood with articulated grain— are paramount. Reinforced concrete allows openings to extend along most of a wall's length and even turn corners without endangering the structure. Floor plans are asymmetrical and less formal; partitions between rooms are minimal; house interior and exterior landscapes flow into each other. This style echoes many elements in traditional Filipino architecture: house parts in the provinces are often textured, and the irregular bent of wooden pillars is celebrated. The frame construction permits large openings and even corner windows. The huge roof and the long windows spread horizontally. Even so, the Prairie Style is novel in its use of the relaxed asymmetrical floor plan and embedded metal framework.

Sometimes it seems that designs of modern Philippine houses seem too close to Wright, but in reality such new styles have enabled Filipino architects to explore possibilities latent in their own tradition. For instance, one of the most famous of Filipino architects, Pablo Antonio Sr., built his family house in the 1950s with a long, low window that turns a corner in his expansive living room. This may allude to Wright, but it also takes its influence from traditional Filipino style. Antonio adds a novel touch: the window becomes a cozy seat, shaded by generous roof eaves that rest on articulated diagonal struts.

The other influence in modern architecture is the "International Style." Inspired by industrialism, it pares down design to its essentials, as in a machine; it proposes that the building should express its intended function. Thus, a house must look like a house, an office like an office; unnecessary surface ornamentation is discouraged. The International Style philosophy states that beauty resides in articulating, honestly and simply, the function of each part, such as the stairs or the doorknob; and that the materials themselves—polished marble, wood, or metal—are in themselves attractive. To emphasize its break with the past, its proponents flatten the roof.

Ultimately, however, Filipinos love a homey look: they do not see a house as a home if the roof is flat, so the International Style has become more popular for office buildings and furniture than for dwellings. Still, some architects like Ed Calma elicit poetry from function. The brick-and-glass house he designed for his uncle, Pablo Calma, opens like a

Japanese fan around a bamboo thicket in an inner courtyard. There are levels and sub-levels. Some levels open into rooms, others into a series of open-air terraces.

The second half of the 20th century saw the emergence of a more contemporary Filipino style. Architects reinterpreted local materials in new and exciting ways. Gray volcanic rock (adobe), abundant around Manila, appeared as cladding for walls; *capiz* shell panes in different patterns were used for various decorative elements; rattan, coconut lumber, and fiber textiles took on new life in paneling. Architects responded to the high humidity and monsoon rains of the tropics with designs that included steeply pitched roofs, high ceilings, minimal wall surfaces, and luxuriant gardens with cooling pools.

At the same time, Filipinos continue to enjoy reinterpreting regional styles. One favorite is the Mediterranean, with its roofs of curved tiles, cheerful stucco walls, iron grilles, and decorated tiles. Another is the Japanese: Sliding *shoji* screens, that may have inspired the ancient sliding shell lattice windows Filipinos grew up with, have returned. Then there are those tiny gardens that bring the outdoors into a Japanese-style interior. And the thick mats for sitting or sleeping on that recall the Filipino's own habits. Lately, a style that borrows elements of Balinese architecture has become popular. Pavilions, with square stone columns and hipped thatch roofs emerging from limpid pools, now appear in private gardens; and holiday homes in *lumbung* or rice granary form and shape are not uncommon.

Postmodernist Style has not been totally ignored either. Postmodernism began as a critique of the International Style's supposed indifference to ornament and context. But since the fascination with historic styles never died out locally—even during the International Style's high noon in the '50s–'80s—local architects have easily adopted, without apology, some postmodernist traits, such as the casual reinterpretation of previous styles.

Other Filipino houses are extremely personal statements. Their owners are not trained architects but simply people who have decided to design their own abodes. They literally dirty their hands with cement and paint, creating designs as they go along. They may rescue worn-out banisters, paint them in vivid colors, and install them on a brick wall decorated with broken pieces of glass and porcelain. Thanks to their keen sense of style, potential kitsch becomes delightful bricolage. Their one-of-a-kind houses reflect the Filipino culture's tolerance for the unconventional.

In this book, we showcase contemporary tropical style in the Philippines in all its manifestations. Variety is key: in reflecting the country's multifarious traditions and the diversity of its individuals, the houses featured are all fascinating examples of Filipino ingenuity and imagination. Enjoy.

# asian fusions & cross currents

There is a growing body of Philippine architecture that is defined by the opening up of buildings to more light and air, an appreciation of natural indigenous materials, and the use of tropical craft techniques and Asian embellishment—all designed to reflect the "modern" Filipino lifestyle. This "fusion-style" probably began to manifest itself in the late 1960s when a nationalist movement in culture and the arts influenced architecture: Spanish-era colonial buildings were re-discovered and restored. Also at this time, orientalism of a local kind cropped up in the revival of interest in Philippine motifs (specifically from the Islamic regions of the country). The result was a type of Creole architecture that combined an inside/outside lifestyle with living areas connected to gardens by a *lanai* (a term of Hawaiian origin), terrace, or verandah (depending on the overall motif: Spanish Mediterranean or California-sprawl).

In the 1980s, affluent Filipinos discovered the pleasures of traveling within Southeast Asia.

Thailand became a much-visited destination and Baan Thai motifs started to appear in Philippine homes as a form of interior embellishment. Bali then became popular, and a "Bali-esque" or "Baan-esque" style emerged in Filipino houses, initially replicating Balinese courtyards and gardens, then eventually the pavilion design of resorts in both Thailand and Bali. Wood was layered over concrete, tile over metal roof, and natural textures over smooth machined finishes. The outside was invited in and the ubiquitous Balinese or Thai garden lamp replaced the Japanese stone garden lamp of the '60s. Parallel to these developments, architects such as the Manosa brothers and Gabby Formoso continued to develop an indigenous style. That style sought to go beyond the superficial use of native materials (even though their experiments with coconut and local woods were commendable in themselves) to create a particularly Filipino style that made extensive use of light and space.

This emerging genre is still defining itself. Most of the newer generation of Filipino architects have either come from extensive work or study stints overseas. They are absorbing and integrating many of the pervading international trends into their still-evolving work in the Philippines. Houses appear lighter and airier; there is a greater use of natural local materials, such as native slates, limestone, and sand stone; and there is more variety in the textures of wood, bamboo in-finishes, and embellishment. Finally, there is a rediscovery of craft techniques in wood joinery and stonework that traces its development to the first millennium buildings in these islands.

All of these tropical-style elements are brought together in a design program that reflects the "modern" Filipino lifestyle: one that is a product of a globalized, even westernized outlook, yet is increasingly appreciative of its deep cultural roots and the richness of its design heritage. It is an evolving style with a thousand years of tradition.
— by Paulo Alcazaren

# hilltop eyrie in mindoro

Puerto Galera, Mindoro, is a laid-back beach resort off the southern coast of Luzon. The town has an ever increasing number of resorts, diving operators, expat residents, and folk-art collectors of Mangyan weavings and crafts. To the far east of the resort areas are Jaime and Bea Zobel's two guest houses, designed by architect Noel Saratan. Don Jaime Zobel de Ayala, industrialist-developer, civic leader, and diplomat, arts-patron and art-photographer, specified "something very rustic, using local materials only" for these two hybrid houses. Both draw on Japanese inspiration and proportions, and make extensive use of *capiz* shell, green slate stone, and cogon grass for thick roof thatching.

In 1996 Saratan conjured a unique hilltop aerie with a spiral staircase leading to a Zen garden. Set within the confines of the Ponderosa Golf Course above Puerto Galera, this 160-sq-m masterwork was inspired by Japanese Zen gardens. Buffeted by the wind at 400 meters above sea level, it has spectacular views in three directions (see right). Set on a 2,000-sq-m plot, but on a 45-degree slope, it is essentially a two-story *bahay kubo* standing nimbly on four-story concrete piling posts sunk two meters into the slope. Cubic in shape, it is topped by a thick cogon roof. Its most celebrated feature is the magnificent stone staircase that spirals down (two circles) to a white-pebbled Zen garden at the base. One crosses to the house itself over a bridge posted with six thick *yakal* trunks. Inside, bamboo pole ceilings hover above walls clad in woven bamboo, and black and brown Mangyan *nito* vine weavings. Japanese slatted wooden screens and Philippine latticed windows of *capiz* shell add to the overall textural symmetry. The linear aesthetic is Japanese, while the earth-brown tones are very Filipino.

The stunning stone staircase (left) spirals down to a white-pebbled Zen garden at the base; set with candles in the early evening, it takes on a magical air. The house walls (above and right) are clad in a skin of interwoven bamboo and the entrance resembles that of a Japanese temple; the structural posts are made from shale rock found in Mindoro. At the bottom of the spiral staircase is a granite water fountain (previous page) by Mexico-based Filipino artist Eduardo Olbes.

Inside (left and below), Saratan's eyrie house impresses with its thoroughly native Philippine symphony of rustic materials. Walls and windows are covered with black and brown *nito* vine-woven panels, made by the Mangyan tribespeople of Mindoro. The vaulted ceiling is clad with bamboo poles and pebble-washed concrete. There are slatted wooden screens and Philippine *capiz* shell windows on all sides.

# beachside guesthouse in mindoro

Three years after Don Jaime Zobel's hilltop house was completed, the Open House guesthouse was brought into being. Set back from the beach front, it is approached by a long wood-plank bridge (above) that crosses a stream dredged for aesthetic purposes. At the end of the bridge rises a pyramid-shaped staircase, with steps on three sides clad with fine slate stone chips. More wooden steps bring the guest into a proscenium-like verandah which adjoins several picturesque bedrooms.

The overall feeling in the architectural details is Japanese. Roof-to-ground posts line all four corners, and outer wall panels of *capiz* shell and wood trellises that swing open are reminiscent of *shoji* screens. On the other hand, the interiors which were designed by Johnny Ramirez have a distinctly vernacular Filipino touch. Plant-life murals cover the walls, giving the house a feeling of rusticity and fecundity. The piece-de-resistance is a six-paneled mural of Mindoro plant life by Emmanuel L. Cordova, while on either side of the *sala* are two bedrooms with heirloom bedsteads. There are four bedrooms in all, each tastefully furnished for weekend guests.

The guesthouse's airy verandah (above) features the six Mindoro palm murals by Emmanuel L. Cordova, as a background setting to plentiful *butakas* (traditional, long-armed plantation chairs). The petite *escritoryo* or traditional writing desk (right) is paired with an unusual seagrass-upholstered armchair designed in Cebu and a wastebin woven of *nito* vine by the neighboring Mangyan tribes of Mindoro. On either side, folding panels of wood-and-*capiz* can be drawn across to provide privacy for the adjoining bedrooms, two of which have heirloom bedsteads: one is an exquisite art-deco "rose" bedstead carved by the sculptor Tampinco in the 1920s; the other (above right) a wide *kamagong* four-poster of American-Shaker style. A third bedroom (far right) in quiet blue-and-white faux-Japanese style has Philippine *abaca* wallpaper and shades.

# tropical rustic

Designer Budji Layug declares that this clay-colored house with dark slate-tiled roof is in "Asian-tropicale style—always tropicale with an 'e'!" and it certainly fuses many elements. His brief was to take the half-finished house-structure and reorient and redesign the architecture and layout. Firstly, he either removed walls or pierced picture-windows into them, generally decompartmentalizing the spaces to let in the light. Then he covered all interior surfaces in smooth, matte-clay tones—to give a feeling of modernity. And lastly, he added the garden: using roughly hewn railway ties and old Cambodian carvings, plus a rustic-Japanese style gate. The result is an all-Asian composition.

The main house approach is clean and modern. Enter the wide door on its asymmetrical pivot, and you are greeted by a reproduction of an Ifugao *pukok* granary, now a reception table. Inside, the space soars to the two-story ceiling, giving the scale and proportion of a much larger house, complete with large glass picture windows high above eye level. A few steps further, and you start to focus on the furnishings and artworks: the *sala* centerpiece is a giant painting by Ben Cabrera, a landmark painter of women in dramatic, swirling robes; it is complemented by large sofas and armchairs covered in *sica*, the inner core of rattan, and touched with ethnic, earthy tropical colors.

Beyond a set of sliding glass doors, is the back *lanai* covered in sleek modern buff tiles. It connects well with the Japanese-style garden. Here, plants have been carefully chosen to provide a mottled shade, cut glare, and soften the modern textures. There is also a guest wing and the entire house is surrounded by a fence of wood *molave* railway ties.

The sleek wooden door (above) turns on an asymmetrical pivot, as one enters what feels like a modern Mexico setting on smooth buff tiles. Everywhere in the Escaño abode one feels Budji's designer touch on the furnishings. (Opposite, clockwise from top left): The back patio is furnished with contemporary armchairs woven of fine rattan *sica* and mixed with Filipino rural furniture. The white-pebbled garden at the front makes a modern Japanese statement with with its dark trellised gate and modernist stone bench. In the bedrooms, comfy occasional chairs have subtle Oriental forms and textures; the guestroom carries the modern rustic theme with deep earth-colors and ethnic tribal weaves from India and Indonesia. The back *lanai* is a medley of ethnic weaves and fabrics.

Bencab's giant modernist painting of two kimonoed women in the high ceilinged *sala* (left). Earthy browns, sepia, and rust tones are echoed in all Budji's tropical furnishings creating a strong pan-Asian statement. The dining area (above) makes an impact like a modern art gallery, guarded on either side by primitive tribal artwork from disparate mountains—Mari Escaño's prized African sculptured figure at left, and a dark-wood *bulol* (rice-god figure) chair at right. (A Fernando Zobel abstract hangs in the light above.) The oval dining table is the longest single-piece *narra* table in this book. Above it hangs an Oriental domed landscape by national artist Arturo Luz.

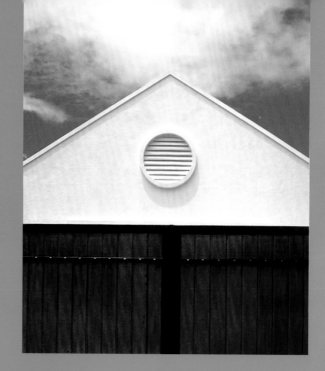

# colonial processional

When architect Manny Miñana had the chance to build a 500-sq-m house to his own dreams and inspirations, he integrated a clean American sensibility with Asian tropical sensitivity. As a conceptual whole, this Ayala Alabang abode reminds one of the Oriental Hotel in Bangkok—all clean and pristine white, with giant trees dominating the space and groupings of rattan furniture among the collonades. Says Miñana: "This is a simple, elemental, conceptual home; an all-white, tropical, contemporary house on the outside, with no moldings and embellishments, and lots of garden." Using a vocabulary learned from Miñana's three Filipino mentors—architects Leandro Locsin, Gabby Formoso, and Bobby Manosa—the house has the feeling of space that dominates the work of Sri Lankan maestro Geoffrey Bawa.

The white bungalow has a "three-layered approach" that culminates with the inner, private quarters. One is drawn inwards seamlessly, entering the front yard and stepping up into an open corridor of white columns, where the orientation is immediately focused down the hallway toward an objet d'art: an excavated, antique jar on a pedestal. Between the columns is the outer *lanai*, set beneath large skylights. This front courtyard is an indoor-outdoor setting of rattan chairs, lush plants, antique furnishings, and a distinctly languid tropical air. Here one senses the passage of time as the light changes through the day—from a creamy glow in the early morning to a deep violet hue at night.

Adjacent to the outer *lanai* and through wood and glass doors is the elegant, modern *sala*. From the sitting area in this room there are views of the invisible-edged swimming pool and the lush side garden. At the other end of the room, the *sala* naturally flows onto the family room, which has another vista of pocket garden as backdrop to the arrangement of daybeds and lounging pillows from Thailand.

(Previous pages) One enters the clean contemporary Alabang house through a colonnade of modern white columns; and steps into the adjacent front *lanai*—a lush indoor-outdoor setting. "The changing light freely entering the space gives spirit to the house," says architect Miñana.

Denise Weldon, Miñana's photographer wife, orchestrates the gracious interiors. The main *sala* (opposite) is a well appointed room with wide floorboards of yellow *narra*, a spirited mix of contemporary and heritage furnishings, and walls of modern art. The long dining room (above) houses a large tropical tree; Lanelle Abueva stone-ware table setting; lush flower arrangements by Mabolo; and an eyecatching monochrome artwork by painter Arturo Luz. Weldon's rustic eclectic artifacts grace the pictorial: a cornhusk lamp by Mitos Cooper of Bacolod (left) and a black Ifugao rice measure, now a vase for fresh white roses.

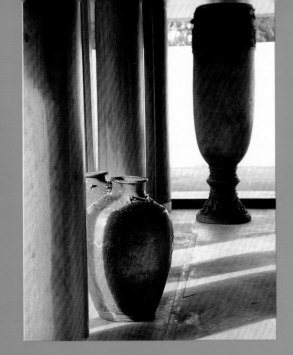

# pan-asian pavilions

"I like to layer the spatial experience of my houses," says Andy Locsin, son of the famous architect Leandro, and, to prove the point, he explains the layers in a house he recently designed for Fernando and Catherine Zobel. The first layer is an all-white one-story blank concrete wall that accosts the visitor and draws him under a tiled canopy to the front door. Past this is the second layer: two cooling pools of differing lengths, open on both sides of the foyer. Inside is the third layer—a vestibule that leads to three pavilions housing a dining room, a living room, and a *lanai*. These are colonnaded, and because they are adjoined by two pools, they appear to float. From the *lanai*, the visitor discovers another layer: to the side of the lot rises another two-story building that houses the private quarters. This building is connected to the living room by a corridor.

The roofs are steeply pitched and covered in flat, dark gray terracotta tiles made in Pampanga province. They rest on concrete pillars wrapped with reddish-brown *narra*. Because the gutter runs across the roof, rather than on its bottom edge, to discharge water into pillar-concealed pipes, the roofline juts in a knife-sharp profile. A pleasant contrast is the off-white sandstone paving.

The house has many Southeast Asian connotations: Recessed triangular arches frame the front door, as in Thai temples (left). The open-colonnaded pavilions, linked together by a central courtyard, echo Balinese palace design. In the middle is a huge, almost-black Indonesian jar. The series of V-shapes formed by the exposed rafters alludes to much of the region's vernacular house ceilings. The two-story private quarters are of white-washed concrete; their sole ornamentation are *narra* panels that extend across the upper story's lower half and envelop the articulated pillars. The contrast between the stark white and the dark roof suggests a Japanese element, but the exposed pillars recall some 19th-century Batangas townhouses that articulate their wooden support-pillars before their cantilevered facades. The postmodernist Locsin says he "permutates" rather than copies elements of admired styles, and, in this house at least, variations on triangular shapes pull the allusions together.

(Previous pages) Multiple layers and levels of transparency and privacy are expressed in this aesthetic composition of wood and glass. Roof profiles and proportions allude to Japanese design, while long, processional corridors are reminiscent of Thailand. Patrician homeowner Fernando Zobel, a "frustrated architect," was intensely involved in the entire design and would have no less for his elegant pan-Asian home.

The project comprises three glass-lined pavilions arrayed separately but serenely amid the expansive Makati property. By night the jewelbox pavilions seem to float on the swimming pool waters. The architectural elements are unified within and by the water: a clear canal surrounds the house by the front door; a reed pond by the edge of the dining room; and the swimming pool that comes to the very edge of the formal *sala*.

# modernist orientations

Despite its minimalist western framework of flat roofs and white polychromy, the residence of Doris Magsaysay-Ho is a tropical courtyard house. Organized around an axial core of three progressively larger spaces, the central courtyard is the focal point from which all spaces radiate. Designed by architect Conrad Onglao, the large, five-bedroomed bungalow (a reworking of an older house) is a safe haven for its owner. The house is entered via a canopied threshold into a courtyard framed around a *koi* pool. Hints of the succeeding spaces are glimpsed through the limbs and foliage of a large pandanus tree and the textured bricolage of stone and wood figures. This hinting of spaces and layers beyond reoccurs throughout the house—a spatial conversation that pleasantly leads one into the house.

The central sanctum is a high-ceilinged living room that branches left and right into the bedroom wing and a dining pavilion. The spaces are liberally accented with pieces from an exquisite collection of Asian artifacts and the paintings of the owner's renowned artist-mother Anita. But the real core of the house is the next space, the central courtyard. Most social activity extends or is visually directed into this space. A geometric pool lined with French limestone sets the stage for and reflects wonderful dinner parties, intimate soirées, or the morning scene of a poolside breakfast under the fauvist purples of bougainvillea blooms. In fact, all the spaces in the house have this connection between outside and inside.

Yin and Yang is mirrored in the contrast of the tropical textures of native hardwood, woven coverings, and cane of furniture against the white flat concrete and glass planes of the house. The palette of spaces Onglao uses allows his client and her guests settings with appropriate levels of sociability, privacy, and intimacy. The house's spaces are further framed by a lush landscape that soothes and calms rather that confines. This is the substance of the house, warmly reflecting the owner's persona and the designer's understanding of it.

(Previous pages): Oriental *feng shui* plays a spirited role in the design. In all directions there are multi-sized water ponds and pools, set with requisite statuary. Out back, a grove of trees and gazebo honors Ganesh within the lush landscape by Ponce Veridiano. The visual focus is a sea-green swimming pool in a courtyard with wide covered terraces looking in from rooms on three sides. Four tall centrally pivoting glass doors lead from one of these terraces into a square, high-ceilinged *sala*. Here, the walls are clad with maplewood and pierced with skylights and picture windows on all sides.

Interiors are elegant and Oriental with modern paintings by Anita Magsaysay-Ho, the owner's mother. Fine prints and paintings and cushioned furniture are enjoyed on the open-air terrace (left)—a non-traditional design notion introduced by LA-experienced designer Conrad Onglao.

# a fusion of styles

The exotic weekend retreat of the Makapugay family is called Casal da Feiticeira or Enchanted Castle. Located on a high spot on the Calatagan highway, the resthouse overlooks the shimmering China Sea and celebrates a fusion of styles: Balinese, colonial Indochine, and certain Portuguese elements. Comprising four cogon-thatched units of differing sizes, all hunched around a dark, stone-lined swimming pool, it has two bedroom suites, a *sala* and dining pavilion, and separate kitchen unit all interconnected by wooden walkways raised three steps off the hot Batangas ground.

The compound was designed by Jun Makapugay, Raul Manzano, and Becky Macapugay Oliveira and is a celebration of rustic-chic architecture combined with stylish interiors. Overlooking the left side of the pool (overleaf) is the wide-open dining room, connected to the *sala* by a brief passage through a Zen garden of white pebbles, crowned by a Thai bodhisattva. The *sala* combines an eclectic mix of traditional Indonesian furniture, while the guest bathroom is an amazing work of shell craftsmanship: thousands of *sigay* (small cowry shells) line the walls and light spills out of giant volutes.

The bedroom pavilions express the tastes of the two separate owners: Manzano stays in a headman's octagonal-shaped loft, while Becky Oliviera, the much-traveled mistress of this picturesque Asian beach manor, stays in the lovely Indochine suite. Every inch speaks of an elegant colonial-chic taste.

(Previous pages) All is Asian, elegant, and eclectic in the main pavilion. The dining room with a balcony over the pool connects to a contemporary Asian sitting room, passing through an oriental "altar" setting: a Zen garden of white pebbles and a Thai bodhisattva blessing all who pass there. The *sala* (above) is an exquisite Pan-Asian mix of traditional Indonesian furnitue with contemporary Western armchairs, antique oriental statuary and accessories with modern Arrakis Oggetti lights suspended overhead—truly an avant-garde accent.

Bedroom interiors express tastes of separate but equally stylish co-owners: For bachelor Manzano, the octagonal headman's loft, a two-story Asian-Javanese unit with masks and spears at the door (opposite, top), complete with four poster bed with Chinese carved headboard; and daybeds and games to play upstairs. For Becky Oliviera, a pure Indochine setting: her four poster bed, custom-made by E. Murio in fine cane, is draped with gauzy curtains, matched with twin black drawer sets and an antique cabinet from the ancestral home.

# bali-mexican fantasy

Situated in Calatagan on the southernmost tip of Batangas province, the weekend home of former Manila Mayor Nemesio Yabut is part-tropical resthouse pavilion and part-southwestern ranch. Built atop a commanding hill, the house glows from a distance: it is newly painted in bright shades of papaya, aqua, and raspberry: refurbished with *nipa* roofing over a massive front verandah; and lit up with hot-colored throw pillows and covers, ceramic jars, and massive modern accents. The interior designer daughter, Gayle Yabut, upkeeps and updates what she calls the family's "modern Filipino-Mediterranean" vacation house (right and page 52). Her own house (see pages 56–59) and the house of her brother (pages 53–55) lie close by—the three dwellings comprise a fanciful fusion of Balinese, Mexican, and African architecture.

On a separate hilltop of the Yabut property is an outré and off-the-wall creation, designed by Nemesio Yabut's son, Ricky. This weekend abode started from a simple pueblo-style bungalow—with organic, rounded wall edges, and rustic wood inserts—and blossomed into a multicolored New Mexican fantasy. From the outside, the house gleams with the bright shades of the main Yabut house—Ricky paints his place in ripe papaya, fuschia-rose, and dijon-mustard, hot fiesta colors that seem to have spilled over to his own hilltop. His longspan rooftop is tinted bronze; his floors are of varnished, polished cement. And all around are the graphic plants that can take the hot Batangas sun: yuccas, sugar palms, and cacti.

The house interiors (above and overleaf) are another story: fashioned by Ricky's cinematic fusions of African adventures and cavemen, Indiana Jones and Georgia O'Keefe, every space has its own theme. And out the back on a wide-open deck—with no rails and an untrammeled view of the peninsula's end and the Straits beyond—are placed his collection of eclectic art-installations. He places a cow skull upon a melon wall and a big white cowboy hat upon a long *molave* trunk (it doesn't blow away, because it's made of concrete). He ropes together deer horns and sheep horns on a *molave* turning post and giant stone grinder: "This works against the evil spirits of Batangas!" laughs the horseman.

Among the walls coated in bold bright colors, there are
whimsical primitive paintings of cavemen (playing polo!);
giant murals of deer in the forest; and decorative accents of
African symbols, animal skins, carved masks, horns and spears,
organic artifacts and ritual sand-paintings called "mud-rugs."

To the left of the main house are Gayle Yabut's quarters: they comprise two small melon-colored pavilions on the hillside, cascading toward the large swimming pool and a magnificent terraced garden of fuchsia bougainvillea. Her unit exudes a stylized Balinese resort air, from the shocking pink ritual umbrella over the outer deck; to the comfy *bale*-cum-*sala*, complete with phone and air-conditioning, day beds for guests, and a music system under the sloped *nipa* roof; to the rustic-chic wickered breakfast nook on the upper level. All her levels are picturesque. Gayle entertains round a "sun-corner" tucked into the steep slope. Here *molave* daybeds covered in fuchsia and gold are set amidst yuccas planted against coral-stone walling. There's an outdoor shower and a technicolor toilet—"where guests can go without having to ascend the hill in the middle of the evening."

Gayle's private rooms comprise an ultra-comfortable, thoroughly contemporary living suite with a raised, hideaway bedroom and all the mod-cons of an urban apartment. Her metropolitan-chic interiors combine natural woods, Cordillera ethnic artifacts, contemporary furniture, and modern abstract paintings by Arturo Luz.

# reworking the vernacular

In the contemporary scene, there are a number of architects that utilize, and sometimes reinterpret, traditional Filipino elements, be they architectural, in the furniture and furnishings, or in the materials. Over the centuries a generic Philippine building style evolved that took into account the surrounding topography, rainfall, humidity, wind, and radiation. For the most part, as in other Southeast Asian countries, these primitive tropical dwellings were built on stilts from either hardwood or bamboo (in the countryside), or wood and stone (in the towns). Generally roofs were steeply pitched, windows were large, to provide adequate ventilation, and public and private spaces were strictly segregated.

In the 20th century, another environmental factor became vitally important—the availability of energy (because buildings, especially those in the tropics, depend on artificial lighting and ventilation systems). Combining the specifications of the environment along with the clients' needs and lifestyles, architects began to reinterpret this

vernacular style. From the 1960s onwards, some new dwellings appeared which were sensitive to the local context and used local styles and materials, but also often combined these with new forms.

A pioneer of this new style was Leandro Locsin who designed the prototype of the modern vernacular house: Rough-hewn volcanic rock as exterior cladding reappeared (left uncoated in order to show off its granular texture, whereas before it
had been coated with lime plaster to protect against water seepage and erosion). Local, oil-finished wood was used in window frames and exposed decorative pillars. Floors of beige marble or granite panels were laid. *Capiz*, the shells traditionally used in window panes, became popular again, but were now used
as a decorative element. For color, designers used combinations inspired by various ethnic groups: examples include Willy Fernandez' upholstery and carpets which echoed the Moslem Maranao's bright

purples, pinks, and mango greens; and the use of weaves from upland groups in Luzon and Mindanao, such as Ifugao cotton blankets with broad white-and-red bands trimmed with indigo stiches, or Tboli *abaca* runners in browns and sienas.

In the 1980s, another phase began. Adobe and *capiz* were replaced by off-white and pastel shades. Recent houses designed by Bobby Manosa use cured split-and-flattened bamboo
in triangles and squares in ceilings, bands of laminated narrow bamboo nodes framing marble floors, and coconut mosaics for fibrous edging. The house-form itself accentuates the roof's steep pitch; a finial crowns the peak and eaves extend downwards. Other architects reinterpret local forms in a more abstract manner. Whether it is noted in the detailing, or in the design of the house as a whole, this chapter introduces some homes that take their inspiration from Filipino vernacular tradition.
– Fernando Nakpil Zialcita

# filipino contemporary

The Paranaque location is one of the charms of interior designer Chelo Hofilena's house: although it is sited in a middle-class neighborhood, one is immediately surprised by the size, space, and design charms of the building. What was an ordinary, '70s family house was expanded five years ago; the result—despite the limited space—is a more versatile home fit for gracious entertaining. The updated design incorporates many vernacular materials such as native bamboo, coconut, and rattan, and opens up large clerestory windows to create a feeling of openess. As architect Francisco "Bobby" Manosa says: "This house has many strong messages to teach regarding Filipino architecture."

The main addition came in the form of a semi-attached open-air pavilion built alongside the original house. This gracious new *lanai* looks on to a jacuzzi pool on one side, and a back garden on the other. There's a bubbly waterfall and tilapia pool behind. Designer lighting from above defines the sloping roofline. The furniture is almost exclusively of Permacane, the laminate rattan product of Eduardo Yrezabal.

The main house has further secret charms. The dining room doubles as a library, whose door panels slide away completely to open up to an outdoor pool with a waterfall. The master bedroom lies back-to-back with the TV lounge, and the television can be swiveled round to face the bed. The upstairs lounge has a mini-balcony/extended deck with a daybed hanging over the tilapia pool! Over the master bedroom is a loft that has been converted into a studio-workspace. The new structures hide storage areas discreetly within the house.

(Previous pages) Interior designer Chelo Hofilena has transformed her modest home into a versatile abode. The main house, with its distinctive Philippine roof-finial, bears many references to the indigenous design of the *bahay kubo* (a native hut), facilitating cross-ventilation and a versatile use of space.

The *lanai* is furnished in all natural textures and indigenous materials (opposite). Philippine crafts are prominently on display: an Ifugao basket for the center table; Mindanao *bolo* baskets in lighted niches; a coconut shell veneered mural; and *capiz* shell accessories fashioned into candle holders (left). A rustic array of bamboo baskets from Palawan and the owner's mother's portrait (above) complement a modern painting of a lady and a bird by Martinez.

# urban organic

Oriented around a huge mango tree, the house of Teodoro and Mercedes Pleno is characterized by an exterior form of sloping roof lines with a lightning-rod finial at the apex of the roof (above) and an interior of vernacular materials. In fact, it is a good example of all-Philippine materials used in a contemporary home and garden. Situated in Ayala Alabang and designed by architect Francisco "Bobby" Manosa, it is an all-Filipino urban house in a vernacular-contemporary style.

Teodoro Pleno, a businessman, specified that only locally available materials could be used, so Manosa uses natural Filipino materials throughout. Laminated bamboo plywood is placed on floors and ceiling-panels; crushed bamboo covers walls or closet surfaces. The master bathroom ceiling features *capiz* shell with backlighting; and wall coverings are made from sugar cane, rice stalks, hemp, and beaten bamboo panels. The natural theme is further echoed in the furniture and furnishings: with the help of interior designer Chelo Hofilena, Mrs. Pleno places live birds and plants and bright modern paintings of them in strategic places, and decorates with all Filipino crafts. Creative tropical furniture in new Permacane rattan is evident; and the owner's fine art colloction includes Philippine classical paintings of early Magsaysay-Ho, Legaspi, Joya, Sanso, and Ang Kiukok.

A grand ornamental garden, landscaped by Ponce Veridiano, surrounds the Pleno house. Extravagantly colorful—like a marine garden on Alabang land—it links the house with the centerpiece mango tree (left). "The tree is the reason we bought the lot," says Pleno. "As soon as we moved here, it started to bloom! It is the point of perspective of the whole house and gives us a feeling of space… it is our lucky tree."

The organic theme is expressed indoors by the furniture and furnishings. Mercedes "Nenen" Pleno—a talented pianist—essayed her love of nature into the house through tropical plants and artworks and plentiful natural materials. The *sala* (above) features "plyboo" panels on the recessed ceiling; a varnished *molave* trunk for a lampstand; and a custom-made console table of white fossil stone on a giant driftwood base (opposite, top right). The artworks, too, extol nature: a giant mural of banana leaves by Isabel Diaz and a painting called "The Enchanted Forest" by Anita Magsaysay-Ho.

In the den and within the niches along the staircase (opposite, below right) are displayed Mrs. Pleno's collection of wood sculptures, all collected along the theme of Mother and Child. On the outdoor patio are a rough-hewn *molave* side table and mortar vase by Osmundo (opposite, bottom left). Nearby, one can see the naturally landscaped swimming pool, lounging deck and the magnificent mango tree—the point of perspective of the Plenos' urban-organic house.

# native-modern harmony

Designer Edong Lazatin describes the style in his Tagaytay townhouse as "Filipino Native Modern," but undoubtedly the foremost attraction is its location—high on a ridge overlooking Taal lake and volcano. A trellis over the front door marks this nature-oriented townhouse, while a narrow back garden with waterfall and pond—visible through all-glass outer walls—wraps the interior with the elements outside. Within, there's lots of light, a high atrium ceiling, and light bisque-colored walls weighted by an accent wall in burnt orange. At center, a giant fish-tail tree soars upwards (right) to the mezzanine bedrooms, lined with traditional wooden *persianas* or slatted windows that look down to the *sala* below. "It is a clean, very contemporary space, but yet it feels so Filipino and comfortable," says a first-time visitor.

In the decor, there is an amalgamation of diverse elements from around Asia that work harmoniously together: exquisite furniture pieces from India and the Philippines (the Indochine colonial look is a particular favorite); cane furniture designed in the bedrooms; hand-woven tribal fabrics from northern Luzon; weaves draped to show off their craftsmanship and natural dyes. The overall effect is of the owner's well-evolved sensibility for natural woods and traditional furniture, orchestrated tastefully in the contemporary idiom. Furnishings are mixed exquisitely with Lazatin's predilection for design books, pre-Columbian pottery, old etchings of Taal Volcano, modern paintings by Gus Albor—and his privacy with the incomparable lakeview.

(Previous page) Edong Lazatin's townhouse's best asset is the cliffside view of Taal Lake and her island volcano. Displayed in the foyer is a slatted wood lounging chair from Bohol; a boat hull sculpture by Dei Jardiniano; and the "fish-tail" potted palm reaching upward to the bedroom level. The stairwell becomes a showcase gallery for a singular piece of Iron Age Philippine-excavated pottery.

Lazatin's distinctive way with natural woods, Filipino cultural materials, and the contemporary idiom gained the attention of Elsa Klensch and CNN's "Style Show" in 1995. The centerpiece of the high-ceilinged *sala* (left) is a rough-hewn solid wood coffeetable crafted by Osmundo. A traditional cane-woven daybed and a white sofa are draped with handwoven ethnic blankets from Abra in Northern Luzon. The dining room (above) features lowland Philippine armchairs in carved *narra* and dark *kamagong* wood; giant murals by abstract artist Gus Albor; and a surrealist work by Delotavo on the burnt orange wall. A primitive Ifugao rice granary called a *pukok* (right) is used as a console table. Within the study, a ritual drum from Mindanao becomes a side-table, while a Chinese apothecary cabinet becomes a handsome bookcase—for Edong's books on art, design, architecture, excavated pottery, and Taal Volcano.

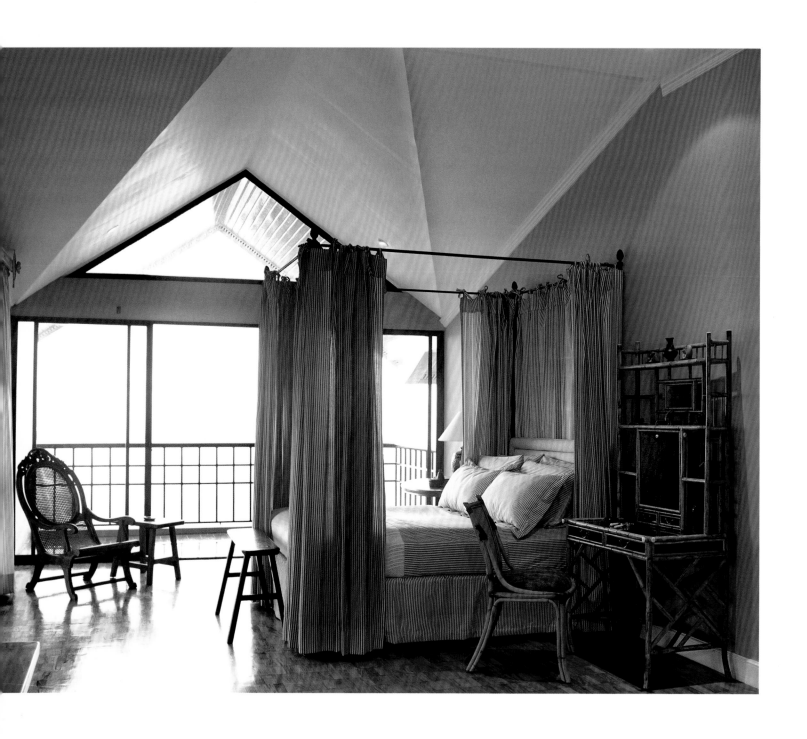

In the master bedroom (above and far right), Filipino *bancos* (benches) and *butakas* (wood and cane-woven armchairs) mix with heavier Indian wood furniture. An old Indian brazier has been recycled into an ottoman and draped with a Tingguian handwoven blanket indigo-dyed with tribal patterns. Nearby (not shown) a *molave* trestle table from Bohol has legs that end in four carved shoes with laces. Crowning the tall windows, over long pin-striped curtains, are finely carved wooden valences copied from an original architectural detail found in Pampanga, Edong Lazatin's floriate province. The Malacca cane and black matting chest of drawers and writing desk by Eduardo Murio evoke a retro-Indochine look: "Murio's cane furniture's scale and refinement work well in our small spaces," says interior designer Johnny Ramirez, who restyled Edong's townhouse for the pictorial. The recessed guest bed (right) is accented with colorful cutboard art by Pardo de Leon.

# the filipino *bahay* reinterpreted

Bernie and Marilen Concepcion's house is a modernist *bahay kubo*—a native Filipino structure expressed in contemporary terms: exposed wood beams under a high sloping roof, sliding windows and latticework throughout, and ethnic artifacts in a concrete, glass, and granite setting. Filipino vernacular forms are reinterpreted in materials of the new millenium. "I'm very nationalistic," says the houseproud Concepcion, a 'frustrated architect.' "I want my Filipino heritage to be in my home!"

Even though Concepcion conjured the look of the house— a high-pitched roof over an enormous *sala*, a walkway across the center of the space for the "floating effect between the bedrooms," and sliding doors all around the lower floor— he employed architectural interior designer, Anton R. Mendoza to realize his vision. The Concepcions wanted to *feel* the garden, to bring the outdoors in, but they didn't want a *lanai*, or open verandah, which would let in the pollution of Makati. Consequently, Mendoza placed solid glass walls and unobtrusive doors to the outside "so you see and feel the garden greenery, but don't smell or breathe it!". Similarly, the owners wanted to screen the house, but did not want to see the screens. Mendoza solved this conundrum with the use of wood latticework, echoing Philippine traditional *capiz* shell window panes, and this became a strong visual element throughout the house. High overhead, Mendoza emphasized the large beams on the ceiling by cladding them with wood.

The sheer size of the interior space is grand—to accommodate Bernie Concepcion's collection of Philippine wood. Old sugar grinders, *molave* pedestals, low rural tables or *dulangs*, wooden ritual drums from Marawi, and even agricultural tools from the farm—all made their way inside. And to complement them, a selection of artworks by Legaspi, Ang Kiukok, Bencab and Luz, leading Filipino artists whose works Mendoza has been collecting since he was twelve.

(Previous pages) The hallway features a wide cantilevered staircase, rounded beams on the high ceiling, Maranao ritual drums, and an Ifugao basket-table on the black granite floors. Latticework echoes the grid pattern of *capiz* shell windows.

Mendoza reflects: "The Concepcions and I worked closely for two years—a very interactive process, they were involved in every decision. I realized their vision and made the owners shine." The gallery-like hall (far right) displays works by Antonio Austria and an Ifugao wood detail. The front door (above) is fully latticed to let in the light. The informal den (right) features an oil painting by Ang Kiukok over a glass-topped mortar-based table.

Mendoza emphasized trusses and beams and used symmetry, glass and ambient lighting to achieve an urban-chic California look. In this grand *sala* or great room, the homeowner wanted a feeling of space and transparency—"I like to see everyone inside my house!" Concepcion declares. Lately, Manila's design-conscious folks have been flocking to visit Bernie and Marilen in their deconstructed modern Filipino *bahay*.

# a rustic love affair

It's a long way from Brittany to Puerto Galera, but such are the romantic lengths that Hubert and Ara d'Aboville have gone to be close to the mountains on their favorite island, Mindoro. The French-Filipino couple were adventurous pioneers of sorts, pursuing their holidays in Mindoro for years, until they found their own plot. Ten hectares of plantation land, lush with greenery and winds whistling through the trees, it is inland, high above sea level, and came with a romantic touch: it was his present to her on their 10th anniversary.

Architect Fernando "Pandot" Ocampo sited the family's *nipa*-thatched weekend *bahay* and kidney-shaped pool just behind the lot's tamarind tree (boding well for native spirits). The house looks out majestically toward the Mindoro Straits. Made from wood and stone, bamboo, and rattan, the house is a simple structure: the lower floor, lined with black *ara-al* stone and *molave* posts, is wrapped with sliding and wood-slatted doors. It accommodates a 10-foot single-plank dining table and a small kitchen, along with an open area for guests and swimming pool users. Upstairs, the giant *sala*-verandah is floored with deep red, polished Vigan tiles and encircled with a continuous *barandilla* (balustrade) made from branches of their coffee trees. Overhead, the ceiling comprises woven panels of *sawali* or beaten bamboo, and the posts are made of natural *molave* wood.

"We bought this land and built this house to be close to nature!" effuses Hubert d'Aboville, an electrical engineer by trade. "I love the woods, forests and big shady trees. I like the cold winds up here, the mist playing among the hills, the light changing on the trees."

Furnishings are all distinctively native, determinedly rustic, and all-Filipino. Hammocks are *de rigueur*; and folksy *batibot* iron chairs, painted a Britanny blue, complete the stylish rustic air. It was originally intended that the main floor be left open over the window sills, but Mindoro's ever-present winds convinced them to add on glass panels. The *lanai* is rimmed with coffee-tree branches. Rooms are wrapped with slatted french window-panels, and bathrooms feature plentiful bamboo, stone, and *capiz*. Ara's favorite reading corner, where the sunlight trickles through the *barandilla* of coffee-tree branches, is fitted with a rattan hammock and a wooden trough of bromiliads. The dining table (above) is a natural hewn solid wood trunk. Bookshelves and screen-dividers are home-designed from bamboo and Mangyan *nito*-weaves. Heavy rattan wicker sofas were designed by Swiss designer Max Kienle; all bamboo furniture is by Australian Richard Dansey.

# pavilion-style living

The house of Oli and Penny Laperal Jr.—designed by Susan Castillo and Ted Narciso of G. Formoso Architects—comprises a series of pavilions organized around a central receiving space. Situated just outside the city center, it fuses various cultural layers of Filipino art and artifact, with an emphasis on texture, timber, and local crafts. Both the structure and the furnishings reflect cultural concerns: The pavilions contain and define a hierarchy of private and social space within a setting that is as natural as one can get this deep in the city.

The approach to the house is through a lushly landscaped, curved rustic timber-stepped pathway and across a *koi*-filled pond. Stepping in, the large skylight above and the seemingly wall-less view of the three pavilions that contain the main functions of the house—the living section (right), a smaller dining pavilion in the middle, and the slightly raised private quarters, gives the entrance an open feel. Connecting all is a continuous verandah; paved in large hardwood planks and rustic granite slabs of varying textures, leading into the garden and yet another smaller pavilion. This small gazebo is built in the southern Philippine Tausug architectural style. Topped with a distinguishing roof finial called *tajuk pasung*, it overlooks a pool fed by waterfalls flowing from a natural stone rockscape. The tropical garden is accented with a variety of endemic palms and flowering shrubs and effectively screens the occupants from the urban concrete-scape of the city outside.

The sleeping pavilion, segregated from the rest of the house, is built as a *torogan*, literally meaning a place to sleep in, from Maranaw in the southern Philippines. It is accented with the traditional ornate and colorful *panolong* (carved wooden details). The bedrooms look out to the garden below and are fitted at the window edge with built-in ledges, as in traditional Philippine houses. Modulated by timber louvers, the windows, again as in traditional Filipino architecture, allow for privacy yet make for a well-lit interior.

(Previous page) The main roof soars over several "formal" pavilion spaces that can be closed off and cooled when needed. The more rustic family sitting areas in between remain open to the tropical elements. When it rains heavily, bamboo shades are lowered from the wide eaves and the rattan furniture is simply moved to the center.

Oli and Penny Laperal head a thoroughly modern Filipino family. They are twin-careered, well-traveled, inclined to entertain friends often, collect modern Filipino art, and have an appreciation of their own culture and Asian roots. All this is expressed in their suburban home with the help of interior designer Robert Lane of Silahis Arts. Filipino art and crafts populate every room and corner: from the multi-colored glass panes wrapped around Penny's basement study (above) to the traditional furniture, carved wooden details, and rural implements displayed by the entrance. A massive wood relief (left) by national artist, Carlos Francisco, is the jewel in the Laperal crown.

The formal dining room (above) is a raised, octagonal-shaped pavilion with wrap-around glass walls, allowing a view of the rolling garden and naturally-landscaped pool down below. From the family's raised private wing (right), the master bedroom looks out toward the entertainment pavilions and the entrance area with high skylights. Philippine modern art is set among old hardwood furnishings: an abstract glass sculpture by Ramon Orlina (right); and an amusing take on the traditional *butaka* lounging chair (left) by national artist Napoleon Abueva.

# urban modern & minimalist

Modernist architecture came late to the Philippines. After World War II architects were re-building Manila in the late art deco style with tinges of internationalism, even though there were a few exceptions to this. Federico Illustre, Angel Nakpil, and Carlos Arguelles worked in clean concrete frameworks with little or no embellishment, but the scarcity of steel and glass made it difficult to construct in a truly modern style. It was only in the early 1960s that this scarcity eased up, and buildings of concrete, steel and aluminum with large glazed surfaces emerged. They tended to be tower and podium complexes, however, rather than residential projects. There were exceptions, though, namely a number of houses built in the manner of Neimeyer, Johnson, Nuetra, and Mies. But many of the construction techniques were difficult to replicate in a tropical setting.

The 1960s saw plenty of clones from American magazines pop up in the landscape. For a while, split-level houses were in vogue, even though the plots of

land were flat; chimneys were also fashionable, though few were functional. At the same time a current of nationalism led to experimentation with vernacular roofs, Filipino motifs and walls, and native hardwood trim cladding in open-plan homes. Another design initiative came from architects experimenting in new technologies. Post-tensioned concrete and pre-fabricated components resulted in some new residential architecture such as single-column structures, geodesic domes, and novelties such as buildings with hyperbolic paraboloid roofs. A notable and successful exception was the Sulu Restaurant by the Mañosa brothers, which used this type of roof as an abstracted native *Maranaw* silhouette. Unfortunately, the structure was lost to fire in the 1970s.

One hot architect of that era was the modernist Lor Calma. His houses were all framed in the angular modernist geometry of white-painted concrete; they had flat roofs, glazed facades orientating away from direct sun and simple interiors featuring plain surfaces with touches of minimalism. Today, his son Ed carries on

in his stylistic footsteps, along with a new generation of architects that includes Bong Recio, Benny Velasco, Anna Sy, and Andy Locsin.

These architects of the new millennium have more access to materials and construction technologies than their predecessors and are also designing for clients more attuned to an urban lifestyle. Velasco stands out with his audacious juxtapositioning of organic and high-tech materials. The young Locsin, like Calma, works in modernist planes and textures but keeps vestiges of his famous father's touch in the materials he chooses. Other emerging architects are pushing the boundaries of what could be called a neo-modernist style to sharpen its viability and acceptability to Filipino clients. The most successful ones ensure that Filipino neo-modernism has its roots in the tropics, and emphasizes a cultural use of space and use of local materials and art and crafts. Most importantly, the designers know when to stop.
– Paulo Alcazaren

# dynamic lines and spaces

Essentially two main structures separated by, and at the same time connected by, a narrow outdoor walkway, fashion entrepreneur Ben Chan's house has fluid lines and curving walls. One unit houses the kitchen/dining area and a large public reception hall. This large, glass-lined hall could be a living area, except at present it is furnished only with a large wooden closet and a bench (right), an art-furniture piece by Claude Tayag. The other structure comprises a studio, with a library, conference table and some giant, stuffed, seat-like black balls, and private quarters upstairs. These are accessed by a cinnabar-red, industrial-designed steel staircase that changes proportion and line as it rises. Says Joey Yupangco, an industrial engineer, about his design for the residence: "Since fashion is about change, I've tried to create a dynamic space with unpredictable form and minimal straight angles."

Instead of extending from wall to wall on a straight plane, the house's wooden floors subtly slant downwards, or upwards, depending on one's vantage point. The dining room ceiling tilts and a Calder-like mobile hangs in perpetual motion. The stairs change abruptly in texture and form, from cement to wood. Textures play upon each other. For instance, in the kitchen, a supporting wall of glass blocks fronting the garden curves around and soars—even as the blocks refract the light —and conjures new shapes. A pebble-wash frame surrounds it. Close by is a straight wall made of bricks. Another wall section comprises plain, cement panels ornamented with "industrial" holes placed at rhythmical uniform distance from each other.

In many ways this is a baroque house, if the baroque can be explained as the style that freed space from the constraints of the box by causing the walls to curve in and out and by fooling the eye with three-dimensional murals. In Chan's house, plane is juxtaposed on curving surface, opaque on translucent. The rooms may be silent, but they move.

(Previous pages) "The house was designed as sculptural art," says Pratt-trained architect Joey Yupangco of this Makati house, completed in 1994. "As the owner Ben Chan is a leader in the fashion world, his personality needs a dynamic space. He constantly seeks change and gets jaded easily. So I have built in more corners—promoting 3-D thinking and discovery of new angles—yet always retaining a tension between the space and the interior objects." Upon entering Yupangco's modern composite, the visitor walks in the open-air hall (bottom left) between two separate reception units. The formal reception (right) is clad with warm *narra* floors, solid wood columns between glass, and a singular modernist bench by Claude Tayag. Notice the Japanese-inspired garden outside; and the uneven ceilings within.

Yupangco explains what he calls the "deconstruction" of the traditional house: "This is a very modern concept, a conglomeration of nine compartments analagous to each other... separate but contingent shells (spaces) that are all flexible in use, and all open to movement and communication between shells." Ben Chan's large private bedroom suite (below) conveys the dynamic treatment of light and line within the space. The floor's slotted opening throws light upward onto the long floating closets. This opening connects visually to the long study-cum-*sala* below, where the owner could conceivably look upon his guests socializing in a lower space. Modern artwork (right) is the center-focus at the head of the stairs: the stark image of "Angst" by Chinese-Filipino painter Ang Kiukok guards Chan's private quarters amid a modernist space of brick and steel, aluminum, cement and glass.

Every corner is a dynamic orchestration of Yupangco's unexpected, modern-industrialist materials. In the sleek and soaring kitchen (far left), a curved wall of glass bricks adjoins the pebble-washed window-frame and wood-paneled ceilings. The designer is creatively playful, using a juxtaposition of materials, elements, and textures in unexpected, unpredictable ways. The intimate mezzanine dining room (left) with window-glassed views toward the bedroom unit is a dynamic concept that utilizes uneven planes and asymmetrical angles to "move" the space around modern designer furniture. A rare, minimalist corner amid a "forced revelation" setting of bare cement and concrete (below) may be used to contemplate an early Manansala sketch.

# organic flamboyance

Architect Benny Velasco's residential design has a hybrid character difficult to place but equally difficult to ignore. His designs have a directness that border on the brutalist modern. In his own house in the eastern suburbs of Manila, he combines a machismo flamboyance with a kind of modernist elegance, or a feeling for material and material to fill up space. His design approach is audacious, and reflects his own personal character.

In all aspects of the architecture and interiors, there is a constant juxtaposition of smooth and textured, stark and subdued. The facade's white windowless walls are framed with outsized plant materials; the matte wall finishes contrast with massive stone megaliths that Velasco nonchalantly strews about at ground level. He even suspends a boulder in mid-air as an entrance archway (see above). Once inside, large, bright-yellow, futuristic columns dominate the main interior room. Spaces are organized around these massive elements and are broken up by them, to produce shifting perspectives. The strategy continues on the mezzanine level.

Velasco exploits the potential of local hardwood and natural stone to add richness and sinuosity to this contemporary setting. The furniture and artwork are eclectic modernist, with strong dashes of color and a sculptural feel. It is a bold and masculine house; even the landscape design exudes a directness that is only softened when viewed at very close range.

Velasco—known for his bold landscaping with giant boulders and graphic plants—uses large organic masses melded with modernist concrete geometry in his own residence's design. He is a modest man who delights in natural things, even keeping a veritable zoo of birds and animals and an ornamental plant farm in Cavite, where he entertains in a colorful Barragan-style farmhouse. He is also a true post-modern designer doing his thing for creative amusement: from the giant boulder raised above the front door (previous page) to the massive yellow Corbusierian columns dominating his home-office, to a bright red window space that is a corner-niche for a rough-hewn sculpture. Every piece is gathered for its organic appeal as much as its function. Velasco collects unique, avant-garde chairs designed with organic lines and modern materials—many by Lor Calma—and gathers modernist buddies who share the same playful sensibility.

# cubist gallery

Lor Calma, co-founder of the Philippine Institute of Interior Design in the 1950s and designer of this house, is very much a 'materials man.' One of his overriding concerns is how one dovetails different materials—wood and concrete, for example—together. His other obsession is in the details, which he describes as "the life of a building." In this classic Bauhaus-style home designed for Mandy and Susanna Eduque, the mastery of materials and detailing is paramount.

The skeletal frame of the house is defined by cubes of differing heights and sizes, and horizontals and right angles dominate throughout. Indeed a somewhat problematic aspect of the house profile is that the pitched roof, a concession to the tropics, is partly hidden by a parapet instead of being articulated. Calma's design combines three materials: white-washed reinforced concrete for the overall structure, pale maple wood for the paneling, and extensive clear glass sheets as curtain walls. To further emphasize horizontals, pi-shaped thin concrete structures rise around the house almost to the parapet's level. They also have a functional purpose, as they partly screen the glass walls from too much sun.

The most public area in the house, the two-story-high living room, houses upper balconies—a favorite Modernist ploy. The pale, glossy maple wood of the doors and the panels mediate between opaque concrete walls and transparent glass. The glass walls allow the main living room space to interpenetrate with that of an adjoining room, a second living room whose ceiling is lower than that of the first by half. The glass also brings in the surrounding garden. Though Calma admires Mies van der Rohe, he tries to soften the latter's somewhat cold look by connecting houses with their gardens. Other softening touches in this house include a slatted wood floor in the second living room and veneered maple wood covering the aluminum-framed large windows.

The front door and entrance make a strong statement for the Eduque house (opposite, top right). Six massive white columms lead one towards the large Balinese carved door "floating" on a wide glass apron. This whole wooden frame pivots open (on a central axis)—and provides instant *feng shui* for the sleek modern structure.

Architect Lor Calma designed this modernist house on a multilayered horizontal axis, and applied cantilevered "flying buttresses" to draw its various parts together. The modern buttresses are seen along the front section and from the back-section, where they connect to Eduque's

bachelor son's unit across the pool. "The architectural materials are the building's ornaments themselves," says the architect of the interiors. The rear spiral stairway (previous page) between the living quarters and the service area below doubles as a display area of antique carpets. As glass serves as interior walls, one can usually see through several rooms to the outside garden. This more formal and intimate *sala* (above), next to a glassed-in piano room, is also an art gallery—for the vast range of Philippine masters from Amorsolo to Zobel. On the carpet is a modern foot-massager by sculptress Julie Lluch. The black metal sculpture outside the niched-corner glass is by architect-designer Lor Calma.

# oriental modern

As the traditional sensibility of the Filipino home-owner often leans toward the decorative, it is refreshing to identify a modern interior that is both minimalist in its concept and Philippine in its content—as is this suite at One Roxas Triangle in Makati. The joke at the new property was that the unit designed by Budji Layug "depicts the Dalai Lama's approach to condo-living!"

The theme of the decor is distinctively "oriental-modern"— illustrating the sophisticated Filipino taste of the new millennium. There's a calm, eastern orderliness and tranquility about the condo; most rooms (except the entrance foyer) have a low-key neutral color palette, highlighted only by selective Filipino modernist artworks. Budji Layug custom-designs every piece of furniture with subtle Chinese-inspired lines—in the merest turn of an arm or the slightest allusion of a baseline. Every piece sits in harmony and is fully integrated with the next. As he says: "The elements must have a balanced combination to make the space work and make you feel you are living in the now." Muted colors speak in hushed tones everywhere—pale olive or taupe—and walls are covered in earth-toned mixes of raffia, straw, jute or bamboo.

Budji has pulled the 330-sq-m space together with a conscious-ness of creating a minimalist space. His spare orientation has left strategic areas unadorned, allowing the free flow of space and the confluence of "quiet Zen corners." He says: "Until I'm satisfied, I edit, erase, delete. I try to eliminate as much as I can, to the point of almost being monastic." There is outstanding Filipino modern art in every room. Budji says: "I feel that modern abstract paintings have an oriental feel— especially the Filipino artists I've chosen for this space." Abstract artworks are centerpieces and dynamic elements of Budji's interiors—not just decorative elements. In fact, the rooms start with the art and turn around them.

(Previous pages) Filipino modern artworks with an oriental feeling drive the *chi*—the energy and spirit—through the Roxas Triangle suite. In the entrance foyer, "Fruition" a crimson abstract painting by Gus Albor, welcomes the visitor; together with "Stone Spirit," a dark marble artwork by Impy Pilapil. A diptych featuring jars and vases by Arturo Luz synchronizes with a high Japanese table. Gilt-glazed stoneware by potter Jon Pettyjohn and silk-and-*piña* serviettes by Silk Cocoon grace the dinner table.

(Left) The earth-toned mural painting entitled "Elements of Dreams" by Gus Albor, works in sublime harmony with Budji Layug's *sala* design. Note the dark natural beauty of the *supa*-wood screen at right. The subtle design of Budji Layug's Chinese-inspired armchair (above) is complemented by oriental bowls and jars.

(Overleaf) (Left, clockwise from top left) Budji incorporates a wide range of indigenous materials and crafts in the suite: bleached coconut-shell in a bamboo food tray; *kamagong* wood and rattan *sica* (the outer core of the vine) in the custom-designed furniture; and more earth-toned, Japanese-inspired stoneware by Jon Pettyjohn. There's also a modern coconut-shell mirror frame by Claude Tayag by the dining area. The serene and meditative master bedroom (top right) is oriented around Lao Lianben's work "Zen Afternoon." The Japanese blue-and-white second bedroom (bottom right), features photo-artworks by Jaime Zobel.

# urban courtyard

Set in the midst of a slew of suburban bungalows, it is a delight to find this two-story, flat-roofed house of brick and glass. Designed by Eduardo Calma, one of a new generation of overseas-trained architects who meld an outwardly western architectural frame with local tradition, the house is modern in structure and materials. However, it is also very much a Filipino house. The lower service floor or *silong* is accessed through sliding doors from street level, while the upper levels or *itaas* are where living and sleeping take place. Stairs and landings are traditionally buffer zones—and so they are in this house.

The main street façade is of textured brick deconstructed at the corner to accent the house entrance to the main upper level. Here, a grand flight of stairs leads to a front porch—and thence into the house itself. Once inside, there is a variegated modulation of light and space framed by large planes of glass, concrete, timber louvers, and hardwood floors. The use of embellishment is restrained, and furniture minimal. The feeling is of geometry and transparency, enhanced by views out to the street and into the courtyard garden. The latter—viewed through an amazing glass wall that stretches the entire elevation of the house—is built around a thick bamboo cluster that rises higher than the building itself. It is a fine example of the Japanese garden technique of *shakkei*, or the "borrowed view." Thus the bamboo becomes an organizing element at all levels; it looks expansive despite the tight site, as the surrounding foliage creates an illusion of depth.

The upper bedroom levels are accessed by a staircase that mimics the entrance staircase. Screened by floating walls, there is again a transitional space before the rooms themselves. At the very top there is yet another outdoor terrace; set amidst the treetops, it is oriented nevertheless around the courtyard garden below.

(Previous pages) The interiors comprise a modernist sculpture with multiple planes of burnished steel and plentiful glass windows looking inward to the central pivotal courtyard. The exterior walls and openings are calculated for aesthetic light entry and provide selective "borrowed views" to both the green of the courtyard and the neighborhood outside.

(Opposite) Four studies in modernist steps and staircases. The spiraling steps descend to the wide ground level housing the cars and service areas. The straight steps (seen here with circus biker painting by Arturo Luz) lead upward to a mezzanine that is the family's study (bookshelves are shown above). A natural skylight illuminates this staircase—which is the main ornamental element of the minimal interior.

# california minimal

From a distance, this weekend resthouse is a simple, modernist two-unit white edifice, gleaming clean and bright against the greenery above Tali Beach, Nasugbu, Batangas. Close up, it is apparent that it comprises two cubic units that are divided by a 16-meter swimming pool. As owner architect Jose Pedro Recio says: "It is a series of boxes with a long lap pool in between." With a wife and daughter who are serious swimmers, the Recios cleanse body and mind in their own laid-back California-modern house and pool, three hours out of town.

The 400 sq-m house gazes out over a low wall toward the sea below. Its exterior profile is spare and modern with minimal embellishment. Lines are sleek, even severe, under a low-pitched, almost flat, roof with no overhangs. The interiors, too, are casual: Sporty, simple, and practical, there is an open-plan kitchen, open living room, and wide open *lanai* which leads to the pool across pebble-wash floors.

The long pool (right and left) defines the resthouse along its strong horizontal axis. A processional entranceway echoes the length of the pool, while linking the two living units. The open walkway is composed of abstract white columns, a row of open-framed windows, and a trellis overhead—making for a fresh tropical approach by a white picket-fenced path. Towering tropical palms form a vital part of the graphic design. "I needed to complete the frame around the pool," says Recio, "so I chose a processional row of Royal Palms, the trees of California avenues. I found some recently and planted them fully mature, as high as the house." The final touch of whimsy comes in the details: low wavy wooden baseboards at the meeting of walls and floors and some tiny brass starfish embedded in the pebble-wash by the poolside "to remind one of the waves down below."

The pebble-washed family *sala* (right) opens to the *lanai* and adjoins an open kitchen. Clarity and simplicity characterize the minimal design (above): glass bricks framing the front door and the wavy detail on wooden baseboards allude to the family's affinity for water and sea, boats and fishing.

# rustic assemblage

Some houses cannot really be categorized. They adhere to no stylistic conventions, but are strong individualistic statements, revealing their owners' idiosyncratic characters. Home designs range from those crowded with unique artworks and rustic-organic materials; to spare, spiritual interiors with a creative installation of natural elements. In all the homes, natural, organic, and traditional materials are married with eclectic ideas and offbeat furnishings.

Two charming examples of rustic assemblages that harken to a *bricolage* style are highlighted: the handmade home of a Borlongan couple that is an eccentric artwork in mosaic tile; and the beach-house-cum-art gallery in Batangas belonging to Ramon and Silvana Diaz.

The combination of different materials must take into account their individual characteristics. *Nipa-* or *cogon-* thatch are outrightly tropical-native, while deep-red Vigan tiles made in Ilocos are traditional. *Molave* wood used in natural-hewn form spells country-rustic; versatile hemp, rattan,

and bamboo are common Philippine building materials. The d'Abovilles' hillside *bahay* in Mindoro is "deliberately rustic, absolutely native, and resolutely Filipino." And architect Wendy Regalado's earthy-minimalist Antipoloan house is a simple space combining inherited Filipiniana art, idiosyncratic ethnic items, and bamboo twig lamps. Today, there's raised consciousness for natural fibers, as developed by fabric designers Yola Perez-Johnson and Dita Sandico-Ong; *abaca* weaves have evolved into soft furnishings for elite homes.

Home-makers often harness ideas during their travels for reorchestration into eclectic fusions later. Ruby Diaz Roa, for example, gathers stylish motifs from Bali, Burma, Turkey, India, and New York and fuses them in Cavite, in the style of Hempel, Starck, Calvin Klein, IM Pei and Adrian Zecha's Aman resorts. Ernest Santiago—furniture-designer and architect, now called Santiago de Laguna—has a very individualistic style. Lately, in his Laguna home and café, Ernest takes inspiration from Ubud in Bali,

and reinterprets tropical-rustic ideas with a modern sense for space and the Filipino love of bright colors. He combines industrial and native materials; favors simple low-tech items for furniture; brings gardens indoors; and plants nature motifs in the artwork. He's tropical-native in his use of thatch; and Mediterranean with his profusion of pillars and bright, modern colors. Every piece of Santiago's furniture is bold, modern, and elemental, created in natural old wood, river-stone and metal.

Also featured are those bemused collectors who personalize their rooms with artful possessions. Says one modern architect, who designs around his artworks and natural light: "Art drives the spirit of the house, defines the character of the home-owners, and gets the *chi* going!" Claude Tayag collects rustic furniture and mixes them with modern art. And gallery owner Alberto Avellana, a master at combining modern-abstract art and found arts, leaves room for wit and humor in his tiny flat.
– Elizabeth V. Reyes

# a recycled marine getaway

This modest cottage in Calatagan, Batangas, is a *nipa*-roofed *bahay kubo* beachhouse decorated with artist Ramon Diaz's ecology murals, and gallery owner Silvana Diaz's found-objects. Called "Banak," the name of a local fish, the cottage is a colorful weekend retreat. The main house is ocher on the outside, periwinkel blue on the inside, and without the usual high walls or locked gates; it is always open to birds, salt air, and friendly people. "We don't have any valuables here, so people respect it," says Silvana. Among the first Manileños to embrace relaxed, nature-loving weekends by Calatagan beach, the Diazes have had the *bahay kubo* since 1983; the thalo blue guest-hut since 1995.

The whole thing is a do-it-yourself assemblage affair: the recycled hardwoods in beams and doors come from old Binondo houses in Manila, while the "staircase" up to the children's private loft is a giant sculptural arrangement of polished *molave* logs of uneven height. The crooked trunk of a *balayong* tree doubles up as the dining table, and overhead, a large technicolor frieze by Ramon illustrates the story of the Philippine Seas, from genesis to marine richness to degeneration. This colorful natural art collection extends to the *lanai*: On display are a giant galleon steering wheel, nautical lamps, a swordfish's skeletal snout, and seashells embedded in the framework of windows, mirrors and counters. Silvana calls it *"pulot-pulot* (pick-up) art": there's a farmer's wooden *araro* (plow) and a carabao harness on the wall; a wooden trough for a fruit bowl; fresh coconuts in a mortar; and big barnacle shells used as accents here and there.

(Previous Page) "I love these bright colors in the Batangas sun!" exclaims Silvana Diaz of their ultra-rustic cottage by the sea. The colorful respite, two-and-a-half hours from their busy urban lives, includes a blue guesthouse with private porch on the beach; and bright pink umbrellas on a sunset shoreline. The *sala* is an open deck on red Vigan tiles and colorful cushions; centered on a centerpiece painting of *Watermelons* by Isabel Diaz, Ramon's New Yorker sister. Two funky figure sculptures are by young artist Duddly Diaz (no relation).

The Diaz couple spend their weekends puttering, painting, swimming, and refashioning the house to their creative delight. The picturesque open yellow kitchen (left) is not as inhabited as the comfy *lanai* (above) where they entertain friends on casual wood benches and throw pillows.

# lumbung hideaway

"I was inspired by all my trips throughout Asia, all the things I have seen everywhere... so I wanted to summarize and express all those designs, while trying to be very Filipino throughout." So says Franco Delgado on the subject of his beach house in Calatagan, a photogenic assemblage of myriad ethnic Asian styles. The structure is a traditional *lumbung* or rice-storage barn, with a definitive, Indonesian roof, now interpreted in local *nipa* thatch. It stands guard over a small pool tiled with natural stone, and has spectacular views over the countryside around.

The lower level comprises an open patio, decorated with white columns (inspired by Aman resorts, Indian temples, and other notions of grandeur), while a wide, raised bamboo deck—for sitting, eating, or napping—reminds one of the Balinese open pavilion or *balé*. A low, square, marble table with recessed space underneath for modern-day legs is set center of the deck. Dining takes place in a smaller pavilion nearby, an open-air affair appointed with Javanese wooden furniture; while outdoor steps lead to the upper levels. Here, a bright and contemporary airconditioned den is decorated with ethnic weaves and artifacts, colorful *abaca*-covered throw pillows, and rattan-weave shades. One floor up a tight spiral staircase (bend as you climb) is the bedroom under the arch of the *lumbung* roof. There's also an upper-upper deck near the *nipa* ceiling, with a narrow space for lounging or for a child to sleep.

(Previous Pages) Franco Delgado calls the property *Cala Perdida*, the Lost Cove, and rationalizes: "I wanted to create a place of my own, where I can be alone, far away from the city and the business." He found his isolated patch of beach on the inner edge of Calatagan, Batangas, far from the madding crowds and elite of the "Tuscany of the Philippines." There he surrounds himself with bamboo woven shades and a private view of both the small pool and the sea.

Delgado's hideaway is a chimera, a unique fusion of one man's own architectural fantasies and wide travels. The lower level comprises an array of colonial white columns and an outdoor staircase, leading to a wraparound deck, for looking out to the seashore of Batangas.

Sleeping is done in an ultra-rustic bedroom under the steep, soaring arch of the *lumbung* roof. There one is ensconced in bamboo floors, raffia, and bamboo window shades, and the scent of thatched *nipa* fronds. *Cala Perdida* is Asian tribal to the core, down to the artifacts and ethnic decor (opposite, clockwise from top left): Philippine shells in coconut bowls; etched wooden containers for lip-wax; a two-toned roll of *abaca* cloth tapestry; and an antique bamboo tube for lime.

# antipoloan creatives

They share vital things: the comforts of nature, cooler air, and wider space. The desire to be away from Manila while owning a view of the metropolis—from a distance. They live in the hills of Antipolo, 50 minutes to the east and 250 meters higher than the sea. What has long been a cool retreat for Manileño urbanites is now home to a new generation of artists. They mix and mingle, sharing company, food, arts guilds—and home-building tips with earthy materials. Count on these artists to lead the way home: to earth, fire, wood, and Philippine ethnic traditions.

Wendy Regalado is the Antipolo architect with a funky streak for designing resin-and-twig lamps out of her backyard bamboo grove. Her rustic family homestead (above & left) has been called "a simple, earthy—and rare—minimalist Filipino home" by one architecture historian. Polished red Vigan tiles warm the floors throughout, while iron-framed glass windows and multiple swing doors open the house to the gardens. The house is furnished with cultural traditions and architectural details (given to her by her writer-mother). There are few walls between rooms—just hangings of colorful ethnic fabrics and a large Ifugao granary door functioning as a divider between the open kitchen and dining space.

Antipolo creatives treasure the old Philippine hardwoods: *narra*, *yakal*, *molave*, *kamagong*—all the shades, sizes and irregular pieces are recycled, re-joined, and reshaped into unique modern furniture and totally hand-carved houses! One architecture-trained furniture designer, Benji Reyes, is building a dream house in Philippine hardwoods—three Asian-style pavilions on platforms descending down the slope of an Antipolo hillside. The multi-roofed house is fully lined with *runo* grass on ceilings (right), and detailed throughout with organically-styled wood fittings.

Artists of Antipolo weave together the natural elements—earth, fire, wood, stone, and paper—with Philippine ethnic traditions. (Opposite, clockwise from top left): A carved wooden *bulol* or ritual figure of the mountains seems to await the completion of Benji Reyes' three-pavilion Antipolo house, a hand-carved masterwork in local woods and natural black *ara-al* stone. A multi-mirrored modern sculpture by Napoleon Abueva hangs proudly among Cordillera ethnic furniture. In an earthy orange bathroom, a washbasin handcrafted by potter Lanelle Abueva takes pride of place. In one corner of architect Wendy Regalado's home, a tall lamp made of tree branches and handmade paper stands in the natural light of an organic lifestyle.

Fashion craftswoman Wendy Maramba has configured her own three-level, 10-sq-m house (above) with red-tiled roof, a seamless window under the roof, a cut-out grid running under the sills like *ventanillas* (small lower windows), and a double-spiral elliptical staircase connecting the levels and promoting good *feng shui*. The main floor comprises a wide space with open kitchen-dining area, open jazz-music area—and a full set of soot-black rustic furniture from the Philippine Cordillera, draped in tribal handwoven fabrics. Modern sculptures by Napoleon Abueva and Ed Castrillo balance her all-ethnic space.

# outre assemblage

The three-story house of Elmer Borlongan and Maria Rosario Bolipata is truly personal. The façade's red brick dressing is decorated here and there with checkerboard patterns in orange and lemon tile; embossed bits and pieces of blue-and-white in rectangles and dots; lace-like iron grilles; white bricks with patterns that recall woven split bamboo; and an occasional plaster frieze with floral motifs. Inside there is a surprise at every turn: The kitchen and the bathrooms cheer up the visitor with their glued murals of broken porcelain plates, colored tubes, and shells. There is a spacious, second-floor roof garden, and furnishings are an eclectic mix.

Designed by the owners, the house was truly a labor of love. They hired an architect for a month to supervise the construction of the building (a reinforced concrete structure) but it was Maria who designed the floor plans and the interiors. Their budget was not large, so they had to scour nearby shops and markets for materials. Items like tiles were bought at different sales, and to make them fit a particular spot, like the stairs, they cracked pieces and glued them together in free-form mosaic patterns. Some bits of glass that resemble the little red fruit, called *mansanita*, they discovered at a shop nearby.

The most delightful part of the house is the second-floor roof garden. Its floor is decorated with pebbles, pink-and-white tiles, and broken red tiles. A chest-high wall runs along the streetside. This hidden sky garden with tamarinds, emerald ferns, bougainvilleas, and ornate metal garden chairs freshens the air while insulating the bedroom from the street.

(Previous Pages) Every house corner is a picturesque story as told by Plet Bolipata's giant Manet-inspired murals. The painters' garrett-studio is tucked on the third level. Below is a quiet nook on the second floor landing, just outside their bedroom wall—which is a colorful grid collage of local architectural details comprising colored glass, wood cutouts, and bannister posts (this page). Opposite, a steep and narrow staircase rises from amid the cornucopia of tiles and portrait-paintings and outre artists' collectibles.

The kitchen (right) as well as the bathrooms are inspired artworks in cracked tiles and plaster. Visual interest and entertainment come from Bolipata's glued murals of broken porcelain plates, colored tubes, and shells—and wooden angels among the pots and flowers.

# fiber-art ateliers

Modern artist-turned-craftswoman, Yola Perez Johnson has created a rustic but gracious home from such natural materials as bamboo, *abaca*, and rattan, a garden space, and a lively imagination. Re-designing the basement of an ordinary apartment in a rambling 1950s Makati house and utilizing its best asset—a spacious backyard—has been a labor of love. Today she and her husband live in what were the servants' quarters, and nurture the spirit of the old mansion with Nature's own materials. Similarly, when Yola's architect daughter, Popi Laudico, moved out—with just one *aparador*, one bed, and a collection of paintings by Roberto Chabet, Jonathan Olazo, and Tam Austria—she reinterpreted her mother's *abaca* fiber arts in her new 95-sq-m, two-level loft. The result is an equally spirited living space (see pages 148-49).

The Johnsons' small *sala* is a rustic black-and-white suite dressed in French doors, *abaca* woven curtains, and Yola's creative touch with textures and textiles. A wide collection of "primitive" ebony-black furniture from the Philippine Cordillera is fitted in white *ramie* upholstery and ivory silken throw pillows. All around are baskets from the Cordillera or ceramic bowls of interesting seeds or pods; design magazines; and abstract modern artworks by Roberto Chabet. The dining room comprises a modern-minimalist two-piece table made of dark and rare *supa* wood; crowned by a fantasy candelabra that is lit by tealights. A vibrant red abstract (above) by Roberto Chabet hangs over a dark table made of rare *supa* wood.

The rustic-romantic touch extends to the outdoors, where Yola has fashioned a picturesque gazebo (right) out of giant bamboo poles and cogon grass. She had carpenters build a 3-sq-m raised pavilion—a Tea House, as she calls it—just one giant step from the *sala*. There she serves coffee on a squat wicker table, lights big scented candles and displays "Amorsolo" —a sun-gold *abaca* fabric by fabric artist Elisa Reyes.

Dining under the trellis (left). On dry evenings under starry skies, Yola transforms her backyard trellis into an idyllic dining setting, graced with fine white tatting cloth from the Visayas and embroidered linens from Taal, Batangas; candles suspended on a metal scale; and a centerpiece of anthuriums among glass balls.

The craftswoman has a knack with natural wood and fabrics. The master bedroom holds two rustic beds (one a *tindalo*-modern; the other old Ifugao); copper-and-silk curtains by Silk Cocoon; and a rural pillow holder called an *almario*. A quiet corner (left) displays a red *t'nalak* lampshade; a cane-woven daybed called a *papag*; and a *baul* (trunk) bearing white lilies. A distinctive Shaker-style *aparador* (cabinet) defines the long corridor and is set under a haunting painting by old master Constancio Bernardo. Yola says: "I love the spare lines in furniture and the torn, natural look in fabrics."

Popi Laudico's new flat is fashioned with the same attention to detail as her mother's. Gauzy *abaca* weave curtains drape the east-facing windows, and also act as "walls" that delineate the spaces within. The "living room" is a wide expanse of thick-woven *abaca* carpet defined by the drapes and veils of *abaca* separating it from the "dining area." The furniture is ethnic, minimal, and modern—three soot-black chairs from the Cordillera. Says Popi of her artistic *abaca* atelier: "The translucent layers delineate the space, without compartmentalizing it. And they let me feel secure—like being under a *kulambo* (mosquito net)."

Yola and Popi's handcrafted furnishings of choice (opposite, clockwise from top left) are: Yola's favorite red-glazed stoneware bowls by Jon Pettyjohn "with a blue comet within." Popi's biggest worldly treasure, the *aparador* (closet), custom-made by Osmundo Gallery. Three sketches by Roberto Chabet. (Three prints in her sitting room are by Jonathan Olazo.) Parts of her 13-piece rustic stoneware tea-set by Pettyjohn. And at the bottom of Popi's spiral staircase to the sleeping loft is an old period-style armchair—found in a junk sale and resuscitated to rustic-elegant glory.

# fine arts and found arts

Gallery-owner Albert Avellana's modest Makati apartment is a good example of ingenious space management. By removing walls, rails, bannisters, and doors, and cutting out large "picture windows" between tiny rooms, he has deconstructed the cramped two-room apartment into a light, versatile space. At the entrance area Avellana has cut open the rooftop over his front parking garage—to shed sunlight on his plants. By lining the garage with bamboo poles, he has transformed it into an open-air patio under the stars. A small foyer of glass bricks around the front door brings light into the house and provides an intermediate entry before the compact *sala*. New translucent sheeting covering the bathroom roof brings in the natural light and the use of curtain-lining fabric as drapes allows for a "billowing in the wind" effect, yet blocks the view from outside. As he says: "Cramped areas have become one continuous space, making room for the real strength of the place—the artworks."

Avellana is especially clever in his adaptations of furniture, which comprise mostly old pieces recycled into creative new uses. An old 1940s' headboard with compartments for pillows and blankets is transformed into a buffet table to stash tableware. A wide mattress is converted into a daybed when he suspends a long cylinder of foam—as backrest—under the window sill.

The main focus, however, is on the artworks that anchor his living space—and the manner in which he installs works alongside natural objects. A mural-sized abstract painting by Lexygius Calip (right) is hung at the top of the tight stairway; it is paired with a rustic "half-sized" *molave* chair. A tiny room composed of inherited pieces (left) is inhabited by a penguin-like sculpture by Alma Quinto. He displays a yellow stone torso sculpture by Pablo Mahinay near a fossil stone found in Iloilo. He pairs his striated stoneware pottery by artist Lilia Lao with a striped beach-rock from Mindoro. A small cabinet is turned upside down to become a coffee table. A fisherman's stool makes a funky guest bench, while a soft sculpture by Alma Quinto makes for a funky guest. "This is one-by-one furnishing, adapted for one-off pieces," Avellana says. "The furniture is not expensive, but I enjoy finding and combining the pieces."

Avellana's *sala* (above) comprises a mini art gallery with billowing drapes made from curtain lining and metal fold-back clips. On display are an acrylic called "Stillness" by painter Lilia Lao; a metal sculpture by Honrado Fernandez; and a dark painting called "Essence" by minimalist Lao Lianben, propped between the canvas chairs. The dining area (left) combines an etched mirror from Lola with an old '40s headboard that's been adapted as a buffet table. The dining gallery by the rust accent wall includes a tryptych titled "Reclining Lady" by Dan Raralio; and a yellow stone torso by Pablo Mahinay. Avellana plays with wit and dualities. He places the obese terracotta "Inday" by Jecky Alano (right) in the newly perforated "viewing window," overlooking the stairwell. Overhead there are wooden figurines among the drapes by Alano and Charlie Co. Three "Little Suites" in acrylic are by Ivy Avellana-Cosio.

# a sybarite's temple

The influence of the island of Bali on architecture and interior design the world over cannot be underestimated. The use of thatching for roofs, bamboo, and wood for structures, and flowers and ornate carvings for interiors has launched a style loosely termed "Balinesque." This style has permeated even to one unlikely spot on the map: Alfonso, Cavite, a modest farming town south of Tagaytay Ridge. Here, a creative businesswoman, Ruby Diaz Roa, has designed a weekend getaway-cum spa-retreat: a Bali-style compound of seven thatched pavilions interconnected by a quadrangle of *cogon*-thatched and white-collonaded walkways.

Built by the spontaneous *tayo-tibag* (erect and dismantle) method, Ruby calls her place "the Farm—a contemporary resthouse done with Asian inspirations and New York taste." In fact, it is a series of interconnected open verandahs, courtyards, raised pavilions, and spa rooms replete with flowers, Buddha statues and an all-pervading romantic air.

A massive Rajasthani-inspired master pavilion, measuring 10m by 15m, has a soaring tropical cogon roof and an all-white composite of white floors, white bed-linens, white overhead fan and white tulle canopy. Two inset sleeping alcoves with carved wooden windows open up to private views of the garden outside. Midway along the cogon-covered collonnade is a two-story Bali-style pavilion with an all-around lounging area (in white-on-white, of course) and a guestroom below. The guest sleeps in the center of the room, with a life-sized Buddha by his head and a black-granite sunken bath (with floor to ceiling picture-windows) and gothic carved doors by artist Gabby Barredo by his feet. Throughout, red roses grace stone grinders as centerpieces in the halls. Processional collonaded walkways highlight selective artworks, artifacts, and altars. When sunset approaches, tea lights in hanging *vitrinas* are lit, adding flickering drama to the setting under the stars.

(Previous Pages) Ruby Roa's resthouse begins at this temple gate. Ruby brought in two Balinese workers to build her front entrance, stone by stone; carving stone walls and farm animals for three weeks. The 20-m passageways between pavilions comprise processional collonades of white square pillars, guiding one toward an artifact or altar. This passage gazes toward a wooden horse, a Tausug ritual figure.

The weekend house is a fantasy, a luxe scene derived from design magazines and travels to fine resorts. Ruby and her artist-sister, Isabel Diaz, designed the day's languor under the mango tree (above). Every chaise longue invites an idyllic setting. White columns and thatched roofs are the basis of their creative lifestyle. Among the columns the Diaz sisters place (opposite, clockwise from top left): a finely carved man-figure by craftsman Caguiat of Paete, Laguna; a stone rice mill usually filled with red roses and fresh white orchids grown by Ruby; a cobalt blue door bought in Bali; and glass-globe *vitrinas* to hold tea lights in the evenings. One editor attributed Ruby's design influences to "the witticism of Anouska Hempel; the immaculate lines and solid colors of designer Calvin Klein; the organic style of Philip Starck; and the Zen minimalism and angularity of Adrian Zecha—master-conceptualizer of the Aman Resorts."

The spacious minimalist bathroom (right) open to lush garden greenery has a wading pool strewn with rose petals and a Buddha on a pedestal. The outer porch of the master suite (below) has a Java-style sofa. Among the hushed-white scenes of sleeping quarters are (far right) the guest bed dressed in fine French silk. It is centered within a wrought iron frame in a stark white room. To one side stands a tall dark Buddha within a blue-light niche. The Indian-inspired master-suite's twin recessed niches with vaulted ceilings and carved wooded windows open out to the greenery—Ruby's way of inspiring a prayerful experience.

# zen & the art of ifugao

Antique dealer Ricky Baylosis has always loved ethnica, from the tribal artifacts of the Philippine Cordillera to primitive arts from Africa. That love, together with a restless creative spirit, has led him to conjure rustic materials into functional works of art. In his tiny flat near Manila Bay—essentially three compact rooms—he displays his own organic furniture and exotic silk weaves in geometric patterns from the Yakans with modern minimalist taste. His versatile designing hands transform castaway items from the fields or the mountains into works of art in the city.

In the compact *sala*, Baylosis displays wooden planks, foam cushions, a few ethnic artifacts, and a gentle attitude for nature installations. The central coffee table is a massive door-size plank of *narra* hardwood, propped on four round stones from Laguna, the province of rivers and streams. Flat, black boards function as paired sofa-daybeds, outfitted with silver-gray covered cushions and backed up by gauzy cheesecloth drapes. On the opposite side, another low-slung plank made of reddish and grainy *kalantas* wood stands upon more riverstones; while a majestic church door from his province of Batangas, now inset with a huge beveled mirror reflects and expands the room space. Tribal wood carvings on pedestals and freshly gathered natural materials—interesting fruits, figurative sculptures, an excavated earthenware jar and sundry silver—comprise arty installations and table settings. On the red table are three ripe miniature papayas and a handful of tiny green mangoes on either side of a fresh flower arrangement (right). A silver lizard and crab are set whimsically among the fruit.

Baylosis started designing organic furniture about three years ago, and lately has been experimenting with modern natural forms for smaller spaces. Whatever he conjures, the Ifugaos carve: "They are the best, most refined wood carvers in the country!" says the dealer-designer.

A personal treasury of wood pieces is assembled into a small guest room (above): a traditional bone-inlaid chest of drawers from Bulacan; a primitive rural *papag* (daybed) draped with a Tausog ethnic blanket; and a massive table-plank of black-and-brown *kamagong* wood. The smooth organic carpet is made of beaten bamboo; and the tripod lamp in the corner, of bamboo sticks and handmade cogon paper. The antiques-dealer and designer has been converting discarded wood into interesting accents for small flats. Sturdy *apitong* wood, blackened by soot

in the Ifugaos' tribal huts, is re-shaped into modern art pieces functioning as chairs. Solid wooden mortars are upturned and reborn as lamp bases. Modular hubs of corn grinders and sugar mills become seats or side tables. The mottled cylinder lampbase under a handmade paper shade (opposite, top left) is recycled from an old ammunitions shell. The bright red handweaving draped over a freeform *kamagong* wood chair (opposite, below left) is a geometric-patterned silk by the Yakans of Basilan.

# holistic homestead

Located in the middle of one of Manila's subdivisions is a Zen-influenced, reinforced concrete house that fuses inside and outside in a simple architectural framework. This layering of space is not unusual in Filipino architecture, but it is the palette of materials used that makes this house so exceptional. The owner Dita Sandico-Ong, a fabric designer, has literally "woven" an extraordinary combination of materials into the design. The driveway of local cobblestone is carried over to the entrance steps, in a larger but friendlier pattern, and past large wooden doors to an inner foyer. This area invites the outside garden in, through the placement of giant picture windows and open passageways, without frames or glass. There is a sensual delight in the sound and sight of running water nearby, as well as from a more distant mountain-view beyond.

Inside is an open-plan, malleable area that combines living, dining, and entertaining spaces. At centre, large *abaca*-covered cushions on bamboo and reed mats are informally grouped on the timber floor. The perimeter is marked by massive rough timbers, doubling as benches and thresholds. There are only a few chosen pieces of furniture along with vertical accent pieces, but all are in timber—textured and tanned in rich complementary hues. The use of diaphanous drapes and bamboo screens allows for further flexibility. The heavy wooden floors and use of fabric as filter and ornament is continued into the more private spaces such as the bedrooms.

As a fabric designer Sandico-Ong experiments with local weaves to create new blends that bring out the textured qualities of banana and pineapple fiber, but still attain the robustness of modern rayon and classic linen. In the design of her house, she has utilized similar processes. Using materials that speak of her philosophical connection with nature, she has created an essentialist-organic style that is reflected in the house's flowing and layered spaces. Neither stark nor unembellished, the house is nonetheless spacious, simple and uncluttered.

(Previous Pages) Dita Sandico-Ong's airy Zen-inspired home merges the indoor and the outdoors with reverence. At dusk, the bamboo bushes look into the large concrete house through giant picture windows without screens, frames, or glass. Within, she celebrates a spiritual life through her creative installations using the five elements. The dining room serves up a clean, modern linearity—composed of blue stoneware by Lanelle Abueva; indigo-and-white chair slipcovers by Ilocos weavers; a bamboo installation called "Tic-Tac-Toe" by Dita's daughter; and modernist ceilings by her engineer-husband Manolo Ong.

Dita's holistic-organic style and the house's flowing spaces (above) invite nature in through windows and wide-open passageways without closures. Her architectural inspirations came from her New-Age aunt, Belen King; and Sri Lankan designer Geoffrey Bawa. Bamboo and paper wall-lamps are by artist Perry Mamaril of Baguio. On the dark stone floor, a native snacks installation is presented on a low *dulang* (table), with buntal tapestry and *runo* grass carpet accompanying.

As a fabric designer Dita experiments with the natural fibers of banana and pineapple plants. As a home-maker, she applies her beautiful fibers to her living spaces. A blue and white woven fabric symphony plays under a backyard trellis (below). The tasselled hammock made of *abaca* rope bears a traditional indigo-dyed horseman-themed blanket from the ethnic Abra region. Three narrow blue and white panels hanging alongside are revival handweaves called *Iloco-abel*.

The master bedroom (right) is dressed with window shades and canopies handwoven of *buntal*, the midrib from the *buri* palm. The white floral throwpillows on the daybed setting (below left) were handpainted by an old friend.

# latin rhythms

Despite the burgeoning American global culture, Filipinos still retain their enthusiasm for Latin ways. For example, even though Spanish names were often replaced by English names or indigenous names after World War II, many Filipinos are again calling their children by Latin-derived names—often names from France and Italy. Similarly, Italian music has its passionate enthusiasts and Filipino teenagers love to sing and dance the latest salsa craze. Food-wise, the Latin preference for garlic, onions, and tomatoes reigns supreme. A similar Latin vein can be seen in Philippine architecture.

The Latin style of construction began in the Philippines after the fire of 1583 convinced the Manileños that it was risky building a city in the native manner, using bamboo and thatch. A Jesuit taught local workmen how to build with stone and tile. Since then, stone churches, houses, and forts in adaptations of different styles prevailing in the West sprang up all over the islands. This intimate link between urbanism and Latinity in Luzon and the

Visayas exists nowhere else in Southeast Asia, for among our neighbors stone monuments were already present prior to Western contact. By the advent of the 20th century, private residences used the new technology of reinforced concrete to sport tall, tile-roofed, vaguely Spanish towers decorated with cartouches and moldings in precast. After the war, young couples still opted for Mediterranean style houses because they seemed "homier" than the cold, clean combinations of plain surfaces, metal frames and lots of glass that characterize the Modern. Since Mexico is also a favorite source of inspiration, we should speak rather of a Latin-influenced style, one that evokes and reinterprets aspects of building styles such as the Provençal, Tuscan, Andalucian, or Mexican. The house of the architect Ramon Antonio features rows of windows with flattened arches that look out into a garden where flat stones in a checkerboard pattern surround an unadorned basin of water with a simple jet fountain. On both sides stand a pair of neo-classic stone urns surmounted by ball-shaped topiaries. Tuscany, which the architect loves to visit, is suggested in a subtle, dignified manner.

Latin-flavored houses exude a warm feeling because of the interplay of strongly tactile textures and curving forms. The walls have a rough texture because of the lavish use of stucco; they may be painted either in white or in pastels. Wall corners and casement edges are somewhat rounded and irregular and arches are common. Tiles—local Machuca in geometric or floral designs, or glazed tiles, or dark red Vigan tiles—either accent or cover surfaces in the public rooms. Furniture made from the superb but vanishing reddish-brown *narra* works effectively with white, stucco walls. Also common in Manila are chairs and chandeliers in wrought iron, for the Spanish past bequeathed a fondness for cutting and joining iron strips together in ornate, spiral designs.
– Fernando Nakpil Zialcita

Roxas House

# mestizo mediterranean

The Philippine *mestizos*—usually of Spanish and Filipino blood—have evolved over the centuries a cosmopolitan lifestyle that draws on their Filipino roots, but nurtures a taste for many things Hispanic or Italianate. An example of this is the architectural style fondly called "Mediterranean." It often refers to a large, airy two-story stucco house, oriented to a patio or garden at the back; it uses colored tiles on the rooftops and floors; wrought iron, arches and slatted windows; and private balconies outside bedrooms wherever possible. The interior layout calls for a high ceilinged *sala* that leads to a formal dining room on one side and opens out back to a covered *lanai*. It is essentially a Mediterranean villa hybridized for the tropics.

The dream of many a well-placed Filipina is to build her own "Mediterranean" house and furnish it with European materials. Mrs. Gina Arnaiz Roxas is one such *mestiza* matron. In conjunction with interior designer, Ivy Almario, she has created a gracious Spanish-Filipino home, combining her collection of Philippine furniture and pottery with a distinctly European flair. The result is an elegant home, dressed in silks and satins, *abaca* and *piña*, with coordinated curtains, fresh flowers, and a silver tea set on display. The most genteel spaces are the entertainment areas: the formal dining room features bamboo-themed wallpaper and fine *abaca*-weave curtains; the intimate Spanish patio alongside sports a colorful tiled water fountain that the Roxases bought in Seville; and the long colonial-furnished *lanai* and dining gazebo on the other side of the pool (right) are perfect for elegant soirées.

(Previous pages) The rustic summer airs of Sevilla waft through the intimate side patio of this elegant house designed by architect Pablo Antonio, Jr. The colorful tiled water fountain was imported from Spain; and the oven-bricks underfoot were drawn from the old sugar centrals of Batangas. The evening view from the dining gazebo (right page); the table is dressed with springtime dinner set by Wedgewood. Flowers by Mabolo. Floriate candelabra by Yola Johnson of Soumak.

The gracious feel of the interior illustrates the way Mrs Roxas and her interior designer worked together. "There was a real creative synergy between us," says Almario. "Gina collects beautiful things and many magazine ideas—and I executed them and pulled them together in the house." The *sala* (above), arrayed under a two-story ceiling and mezzanine. The elegant dining room (at right) is lined in a fine French bamboo-themed wallpaper and trimmed with curtains made of Philippine *abaca*-weave by Soumak. The well-tailored bedrooms (opposite) are all coordinated with finest French prints, English cottons, and Thai silks—selected for their colonial-tropical themes.

The *lanai* at the back of the house is the perfect spot for
enjoying the morning sunlight or night-time starshine. Here
are arrayed a lively selection of contemporary Western sofas
mixed with heirloom Anglo-Indian plantation furniture. "I like
colonial-period Asian furniture, because it blends easily with
the European pieces," says the collector Gina Roxas. There are
also large seagrass armchairs by Primafil; a colonial Indian baby
crib turned into a coffeetable; and an antique rocking horse
from Paete, Laguna. In one corner (right) Gina displays her
collection of Metal Age excavated pottery—"the Philippines'
oldest art form." On the right side of the *lanai* (opposite) a
massive 18th-century *capiya* or wooden church bench serves for
afternoon tea. The embossed silver candlestand is made from
*remelletes*, the beaten silver ornaments found on church altars or
carriages. Red lacquerware containers from Burma. Melon-dyed
sisal rug from Borders.

# malate moderne

In pre-war Manila, the Malate district by the bay, full of grand villas and art-deco apartments, was *the* area to live. One jazz-age structure still survives and is home to a newer generation that has re-discovered life in the city. Commissioned by Dr. Manuel Tuason to a design by Cornell-trained American architect, Cheri Mandelbaum, the Rosaria Apartments were built during the 1930s in the new "moderne" style. Finished in 1936, the block had all the latest conveniences, such as elevators and central air-conditioning. Post-war, it managed to fend off the effects of urban decay until the area's current revival and gentrification. Living above all of this, in the penthouse of the Rosaria, is the family of Franco and Rose Marie T. Delgado, both classic, house-proud designers.

The Delgados' apartment is the result of over two decades of refinement. Mandelbaum's original design was commodious and functional, with large windows bringing light in to the high-ceilinged rooms. The Delgados improved on this solid base by first merging two apartments and eventually adding a top floor. The expanded living area from one apartment leads into a series of spaces that flow from an inviting ante-*sala* to several sitting areas—all integrated with the rich texture of the couple's art collection of Filipino masters. Solid hardwood floors contrast well against marble and specially woven carpets. The formal dining room is a few steps up. The bedrooms and study, in the adjoining wing, are furnished less formally in rattan, weave, and native fiber matting.

A spiral stairway (right)—complete with exquisite detailing in keeping with the apartment's original craftsmanship—leads from the entrance vestibule up to the second level. This floor contains an entertainment area, a guestroom, and the kitchen, which connects both to the formal dining room below as well as to the outdoor patio. Generally more rustic in character, this upper floor is dominated by the bougainvillea-clad trellised terrace with an outdoor bar. From here, one can still glimpse the pre-war parts of Malate and take in a panoramic view over the famous Manila bay.

(Previous Pages) Rose Toda Delgado, resident of this family treasure since 1974 and manager of the heritage building, directs the continuous expansion of the apartment. The couple's very first heirloom piece is a wood-inlaid Batangas *aparador* (closet) with a carved crown (left above)—placed within a perfect niche (the original living rooms had a touch of American East Coast by way of this allusion to a fireplace on an inner wall.) Displayed by the grand entrance staircase (right) are a Tibetan *thangka* and a splended Chinese jade collection. At left below is a reading nook by a tall window at the top of the double-spiral stairs on the fifth floor.

The main living areas (left) comprise a series of spaces that flow and interconnect seamlessly, even as they are landmarked with an art collection of Filipino masters—starting with a Fernando Amorsolo landscape (opposite) above the scarlet sofa. Today the apartment has a Spanish-style patio that's cool in summer and superb at night (above); and a comfy family-lounge (left, below) comprising rattan chairs and rustic bamboo window shades. Easily one of Rose's favorite spots is the sun-lit Oriental corner (right) between a Buddha and an ancestral portrait of the Empress Dowager.

(Opposite, clockwise from top left): A Chinoiserie tapestry-mural, hung between the Delgados' winding staircases, shows how the French colonialists viewed life in old China. An old Dutch lamp throws porcelain light on a dark wood *baul* (trunk) from Batangas. Along the hallway are two relief-carved Ifugao house-panels straddling a small wood-slatted bench. The carved mirror frame is from the Visayas. The naif painting is by a young artist named Henri. In a *sala* corner is a rustic table of loose bamboo sticks.

The formal dining room (above) is embellished with both modern and classical Chinese art pieces, the prominent colors are gold, orange, and beige set off by a distinctive sea-green carpet. The centerpiece is a heavy Philippine hardwood table with a patterned top. In the adjoining wing, the bedrooms and study are furnished less formally in rattan and weave in styles that move from pre-war, curved cane art deco to the contemporary resort-style chaise lounges in native fiber matting.

# east-west sensitivities

Slender, flattened round arches, sometimes misleadingly called tudor, define the house of Ramon Antonio. Rows of these, opening like palm trees, make up the windows; large arches with narrow, stylized columns form the doors. They give the house a dignified, but relaxed, feel. They also say something about the owner's artistic orientation. Drawn to Latin Europe, he travels regularly to Italy and loves Paris and Barcelona. But he is equally fond of East Asia and takes his rows of colonial arches from Singapore's Raffles Hotel and the traditional shophouses of the Straits Chinese.

Antonio's prime influence was his father Pablo Antonio, one of the pioneers of modern Filipino architecture. Conversations at home often revolved around art, while free time was spent with his father on construction sites and in hardware stores. The elder Antonio's buildings are elegant structures, carefully oriented to maximize air flow, thus eminently well-suited to the tropics. Elegance, airiness and practicality characterize his son's houses as well. "I try not to depend on air-conditioning and artificial lighting," he says. "Moreover, I am inclined to a more modern style, while avoiding mere trendiness." The drawing room (right) illustrates this well: The walls are white, the floor of light Philippine marble, and light and air gently suffuse the room. The subtle leaps of the arches soften the room's simple style, and because they focus the eye on the garden door, they make the room seem larger than it really is.

The decor reflects Antonio's Latin-East Asian orientation: minimalist chairs by Mario Botta are placed adjacent black chairs and white tables by Philippe Starck. Northern Chinese tables made of *hong* or black-wood stand by a fine Chinese food cabinet and Ming-style horseshoe chairs. All are drawn together by a sensitive color palette: blacks and off-whites with occasional objects in silver, the owner's preferred precious metal. Samples of Philippine modern art, like Luz and Albor paintings, emphasize the linear, black-and-white combinations he likes. For accent, one sofa is upholstered in bright peach red—to match the strong red painting by Arturo Luz that greets the visitor at the house entrance (see page 187).

(Previous pages) On the *sala's* north side a wide door frames
an unusual glass table (inspired by a bamboo fish-trap) before
it opens out to a sprawling Italian-inspired garden. The dinner
setting is placed upon a classic '50s wrought-iron garden set
by Manila-based designer Ernst Korneld. The house itself
demonstrates the architect's Mediterranean-inspired approach
to architecture, although as he says himself he is now "more
inclined to a modern and minimalist style."

The drawing room (above) illustrates Antonio's love for
tropical light and the allure of colonial arches of Straits
Chinese shophouses. At ground level there are large picture
windows; an eclectic array of designer-furniture—minimalist
chairs by Mario Botta; modern chairs and tables by Philippe
Starck; and Ming-style horseshoe chairs. An 18th-century
Shan Buddha anchors the *sala,* and a peach-red sofa accents
the room. An oriental luncheon room (right) looks out to the
garden greenery and faux-walls of latticework. "Architecture
is about creating the illusion of space in small areas," he says.

The upper floor rooms have fine slatted windows—locally called *persianas*—within their flattened round arches (right), hearkening again to Antonio's avowed taste for suffused light and the refined "Raffles look." Art objects include stone Buddha heads and blue-and-white ceramics, Chinese furniture pieces and his favorite collections of ornate silver items and candles. "One must enjoy one's home, be comfortable in gracious living," the elegant eclectic says. "Collected things make the personality of the home."

The decor reflects a sophisticated marriage of East and West—as Antonio mixes tactile textures, materials, and designs; and matches traditional Philippine furniture with modern Filipino art. His blue-and-white den (above) revolves around a striking abstract painting by modernist Gus Albor. (Opposite, clockwise from top left): The small glass budvase was picked up in a London shop; black-wood tray with fine bamboo weave is from China. Two bone-inlaid wood cabinets are Filipiniana heirloom pieces from Baliuag, Bulacan. Blue optical painting is by modernist Romulo Olazo. Linear red painting by National Artist Arturo Luz is paired with two red Burmese *sounuks* or lacquered offering jars.

# hispanic flair

Though a business executive like his father Enrique, Inigo Zobel loves to design houses. In this, his latest two-story abode, he is ably assisted by his wife Maricris. Relating to both the physical environment and the country's traditions, the house pulls elements of old Manila and combines these with a fiery Hispanic flair. There are generous doors and windows throughout, creating an airy feeling typical of traditional Filipino houses. Stained-glass windows with geometric designs, executed by Kraut, a Manila institution since the 1900s, illuminate the stairwell. Multiple matching wooden doors featuring engraved fleurettes came from a demolished 19th-century Manila house. True to the spirit of the Spanish Mediterranean littoral where they vacation regularly, the Zobels love strong colors and confidently express this both inside and outside.

One enters the house into a narrow hall with large windows and built-in seats. This leads onto a dramatic living room with wide *narra* planks, tribal carpets, and rust-colored walls —surrounding furniture richly upholstered in turquoise and mahogany tones. These rich shades form a striking setting for a large, bold abstraction of Japanese geishas by painter Ben Cabrera (see page 191)—from whose artwork Maricris picked up the rust tones for her walls. Other rooms are painted in strong but soothing colors: grass-green for one, sea-blue for another. The living room is lined with large doors that open easily to a wide *lanai* running beside the garden. Though there is a formal dining room with a chandelier, the Zobels usually dine in the outdoor *lanai* on Budji-designed furniture. Across the garden, stone steps lead to an elevated pool dominated by a Balinese *balé*. The entire pool and pond complex—a wondrous setting by night—was designed by Bali-based landscaper Made Wijaya.

The exterior of this concrete house is coated with smashed clay painted in light orange. It has a high-pitched roof with wide eaves, a sensible response to tropical conditions. The house is located in Makati, an area that was mostly grassland outside Manila until the 1950s. But the Ayalas, who owned this grassland, commissioned a new city here with broad avenues, high-rise office buildings, and residential areas. It was a success, and many of the houses in this book are in the area.

(Previous Pages) Inigo and Maricris Zobel's latest two-story, concrete house feels proudly Hispanic with its terracotta colors, tile roof with wide eaves, and the stairway-tower's art-deco, stained-glass windows (pictured here on right). The front door (left) is the largest among multiple, etched wooden doors recycled from an old Binondo, Manila, house. The regal dining room centerpiece (top) is framed with tropical curtains from France and raffia shades by Soumak.

The Zobel foyer (a Tuscan-style silver-finished dome) leads to a sunny carpeted hall (left) with large windows. At the far end are Inigo and his artist-mother Rocio, in a portrait by Claudio Bravo. The interiors were dressed and furnished by Maricris Cardenas Zobel with Ben Hughes of Steven Leach. "I like the colors and style of southern Spain, combined with this rich Turkish feeling," says Maricris, who claims a Mexican-Filipino bloodline. Modern artworks in the corner (right) are by Inigo's uncle, minimalist painter Fernando Zobel, and the Filipino cubist Malang.

The *sala* opens to a wide, comfortable *lanai* (above) clad in ocher-toned Turkish limestone tiles and Asian tropical furnishings. The owners entertain on this relaxed verandah among rattan-weave sofas and Chinese artifacts and accents. Across the back yard is a long, elevated pool dominated by a Balinese *balé*, a watery complex (opposite) that transforms into an idyllic setting by night.

# furnishing index

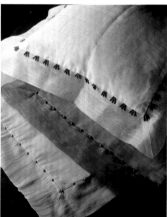

Araceli Pinto Mansor, executive director of CITEM, the Philippine trade expositions center, has been nurturing the furniture export market by exposing local designers to global tastes, while giving manufacturers an annual venue in which to show, exchange, and uplift design sensibilities. After a decade of furniture expositions, the Philippines has been dubbed the "Milan of Asia" by one enthused foreign buyer.

International recognition of local designers started in the fall of 1999 when the Philippines' design-team called "Movement 8" was the hit of a furnishing exhibition in Valencia, Spain. Eight Filipino designers, who exhibited their innovative modern furnishings with all-natural textures, startled the trade and put the country's name on the world furnishings map. As Mansor says: "Our designers use natural materials such as *abaca*, paper pulp, leather, wood, rattan and metal. But technology and handicraft merge: our products have the sensitivity of the hand-

made along with the technology. It's a difficult balance, but our products have soul!" Designer Budji Layug, Mansor's creative partner in Movement 8, knows well the constant need to innovate and create unique furnishings: "We can only excel in the world market through our dynamic creativity—by re-designing high-end, handmade furnishings."

We feature here a visual celebration of Philippine crafts and furniture created from a wide range of natural materials. Contemporary designs in native materials—from hardwood and hemp, to clay, paper and natural fabric; to bamboo and rattan. We look at fine craftsmanship with organic materials; note the artistry in stone, marble, pottery, recycled wood. We focus especially on Philippine furniture of the eclectic and minimal kind; and appreciate the understatement in design that respects the nature of the material. We cite the myriad designs emerging from Manila and Cebu—all celebrating the Filipinos' soulful creativity with natural materials.
– Elizabeth V. Reyes

# abaca

**1** Red *t'nalak* pillows—handloomed *abaca*-weave with coco-bead trimmings. Design: Mandaya Weavers of Davao. Courtesy: Catherine Zobel. **2** Jumbo-*abaca* rugs; Yola Perez Johnson has a patent on the herringbone pattern in *abaca* carpets; Zebra or Tamaraw models. Courtesy: Soumak. **3** Three tones of *abaca* rugs: negra, white, and natural *abaca*, handwoven Bicol. Design: Yola of Soumak. **4** *Abaca pinukpok* cloth—finest *abaca* threads are hand-loomed and embroidered as fabric fit for a *barong*. Design: Herminia Weaving Center, Iloilo. **5** *Abaca negra*—the black-dyed fiber rug called Tamaraw. Design: Yola of Soumak. **6** Banana-linen covers—all natural hues of *abaca* fabric are sewn into throw pillow covers, with coconut shell buttons. Courtesy: Dita Sandico-Ong. **7** Banana-rayon covers—fine banana fiber is mixed with rayon threads, dyed flourescent colors for throw pillows. Design: Elisa Reyes. **8** *Ticog* rugs—native jute is woven into light rugs of two earth-brown tones. Courtesy: Soumak.

A wide range of matting materials is available in natural seagrass; sisal (*Agave sisilana*); coir from the coconut husk; jute; and *abaca*, a banana fiber better known as Manila hemp. Most of these fibers are quite rough, thick and have dirt-shedding qualities—great for the natural, organic look in a house. The tropical hemp plant or *Agave abaca*, originally used to make sturdy ship's rope, has been revived, innovated, and elevated into rustic-chic products for elite Filipino *lanais* and *salas*. With specialized handling and long hours of manual dexterity, the versatile *abaca* fiber can be woven into classy carpets in herringbone weaves and duotone patterns—tropical hemp rugs that are highly regarded in upscale markets. "*Abaca* is the strongest, most versatile fiber in the world," says Yola Perez, a designer of handmade, "jumbo" *abaca* rugs in her patented herringbone weave. "Every piece is a unique work of art with only one person weaving the whole thing, so the design is consistent throughout." *Abaca* can also be dressy, with the finest threads of the *abaca* plant carefully selected, stripped, beaten to softness (called "*pinukpok*"), hand-woven and embroidered into fine dress fabrics. Natural *abaca* fiber is also woven into voluminous and translucent curtain fabrics. Fabric-designer Dita Sandico-Ong has been developing organic fabrics—earth-friendly, dyed natural cloths—by combining banana (*abaca*) and pineapple (*piña*) fibers with more conventional rayon and linen threads for vibrant sheen and rich textures.

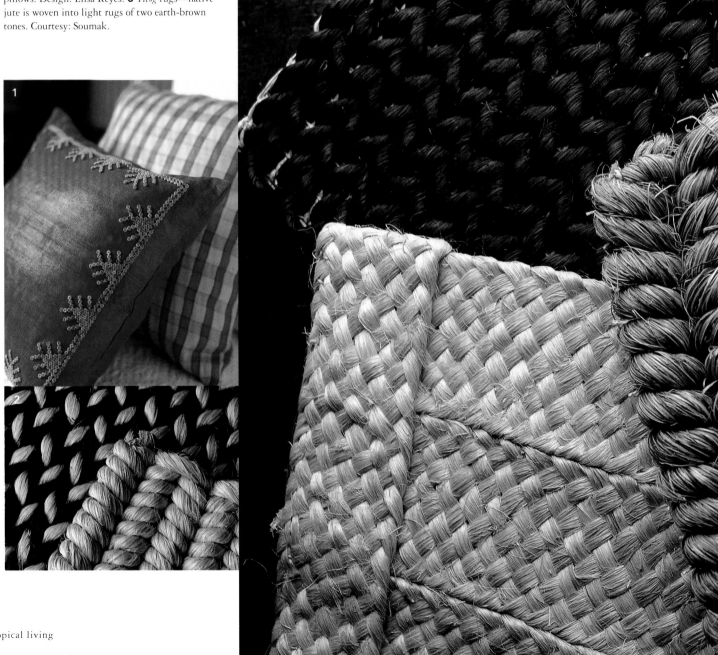

# bamboo

**1** Bamboo sleigh bed—contemporary design features beaten bamboo panels on the headboard and footboard. Design: Dem Bitantes for Designs Ligna, Manila. **2** *Kawayan aparador* (bamboo cabinet)—a rustic classic made of raw bamboo poles and panels, with a manual locking system. An heirloom piece by Richard Dansey of Danscor. Collection: Ara d'Aboville. **3** *Runo* table, chair, and screen divider—sturdy furniture from Sagada, Bontoc. Courtesy: Galerie Dominique. **4** "Gabi loveseat"—a bamboo sofa with freeform bamboo pole backrest. Design: Polymart. Modern red *ikat*-woven blanket by Narda's Ikat. **5** Galleon loveseat—rustic seat made of giant bamboo poles tied with *abaca* rope; with matching Galleon coffee-table. Design: Polymart. Modern *t'nalak* dyed-*abaca* pillow-cover, courtesy: Galerie Dominique. **6** Bamboo armchair—modern chair incorporates beaten-bamboo veneer on seat-back. Design: Budji Layug. **7** Angular loveseat—sofa in bamboo-laminated frame with silver-leafed legs. Design: Murillo's Export of Cebu. **8** *Gallinera* table originally designed for storing live chickens, with matching bamboo seats. Design: Richard Dansey of Danscor. Courtesy: Ara d'Aboville. **9** Bamboo-laminated tray; and twig-wrapped vigil candles. Made in Bacolod, Negros. Courtesy: Tesoro's, Makati.

The most rustic natural material, bamboo has had a great revitalization in recent years. Where once the bamboo—miracle material of Asia—was associated only with rural housing and urban scaffolding, today it is the cachet of natural design. Strong and light, with tensile strength greater than steel, this versatile, fast-growing grass, with its hollow pole and waterproof outer skin, is turned into containers and utensils of all types; into rural furniture or lightweight accessories; into woven panels called *sawali* for dividers; or into laminated bamboo panels called "plyboo," newly manufactured for walls and floors. Filipino designers today are beating it, shaving it, stripping, varnishing, and reweaving its skin—to produce warm organic veneers for modern furniture. Designer Budji Layug popularized a line of giant bamboo armchairs in the early '80s; by the mid-'90s, Richard Dansey—today's bamboo-enamoured manufacturer—harnessed whole bamboo poles in their natural form to produce unique bamboo furnishings fit as global heirlooms. Furthermore, many modern furniture designers such as Bernie Sason use crushed bamboo as an appliqué veneer.

# baskets & vines

**1** Warm plate-tray and trivet—made of coiled seagrass, by Soumak. **2** Open-weave bread baskets made of *baging*, a wild vine from the Cordillera Mountains. Courtesy: Soumak. **3** *Nito* vine woven basket for fruit, bread or sundries. Courtesy: Soumak. **4** Giant *nito* basket as clothes' hamper, designed and made by native Iraya Mangyan weavers of Mindoro. Courtesy: Ara d'Aboville. **5** Beaten stainless silver flatware and plate; over a *nito*-coiled sewing basket. Courtesy: Soumak. **6** *Nito*-weave jewelry boxes in a carved ornamental wooden tray. Coutesy: Soumak. **7** *Duyan* chair— varnished rattan-weave native hammock on wrought iron stand. Design: Robert Lane of Silahis Crafts.

Indigenous crafts designer Robert Lane extols Philippine materials and baskets: "The natural materials for crafts are common to Southeast Asia—but the Filipinos are the most *creative* in designing with those materials. Here, bowls can be made out of everything: *buri* palm, *nito*, even paper! When it's a bad year for hemp, we can make rope out of bamboo twisted together. Creative design with natural materials is our forte!" Reeds, grasses, and palms—the variety is tremendous—await management and processing. Grasses and vines for furnishings are collected from the wild or from plantations; *anahaw* and *nipa* palms are dried and sewn into thatched shelter materials; seagrasses and water grass go into trays and coasters. Brown-toned *nito* vine, woven by the adept hands of Iraya Mangyans, is coiled into practical baskets and jars for everyday tropical living. One common palm that has seen modern use is the *buri* palm: the dried white leaves transform into native *raffia* straw. Finally, the winding rattan vine: its inner core can be plaited into a lightweight bowl; its long strands can be split into wicker—which is woven into a rustic hammock called a *duyan*; or tilted on a metal frame to transform into Lane's *duyan* chair.

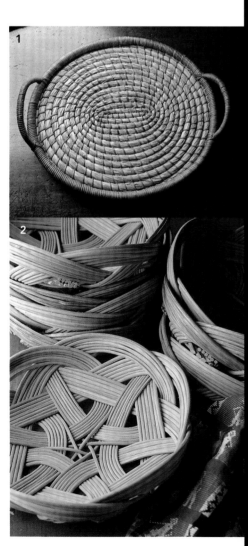

# capiz, piña & philippine silk

**1** *Capiz*-laminate oval placemats. Courtesy: Tesoro's, Makati. **2** *Capiz* shell photo frames. Courtesy: Tesoro's, Makati. **3** Mother-of-Pearl plate. Courtesy: Tesoro's, Makati. **4** Philippine silk-draped bamboo bed—*abaca*-and-silk-net canopy, silk bedspread and pillowcases of Neilino Silk. Courtesy: Jeanne Goulbourn of Silk Cocoon. Photo by Tom Epperson. **5** Dyed *t'nalak-abaca* pillow covers with coco-bead trimmings. Design: La Herminia Weaving of Kalibo, Aklan. **6** *Piña*-draped bed—diaphanous bedcovers are of pure pineapple fabric from Kalibo, Aklan, over pure Chinese silk lining. Curtains are Neilino silk-and-*abaca* fabric by Silk Cocoon. Courtesy: Doris Ho. **7** "Princess" *capiz* lamp—a Tiffany-style hanging lamp in *capiz* shell and wood. Design: Palayan Lamps. **8** Shell-veneered jewelry boxes—white troca shell, brown pen and Philippine jade boxes are unique crafts. Courtesy: Tesoro's, Makati. **9** *Abaca* curtains—voluminous dining room drapery made of fine *abaca* weave with raffia trimming. Design: Soumak. Courtesy: Gina Roxas.

A fondness for the translucent is a vital aspect of Filipino style. Filipinos choose gauzy over opaque; delicate materials that reveal rather than conceal; fine fabrics or traceries that mute forms and colors. The endemic *capiz* shell is a common bivalve mollusk originally from the province of Capiz on Panay Island; its primary use was within the grids of wood-latticed windows in traditional Filipino houses, but today it emerges in the form of placemats, frames, lampshades, and lightboxes. *Piña* is the fine yet sturdy thread derived from a wild red pineapple plant from Panay. *Piña*-cloth weaving—where fibers are hand-stripped from native "Bisaya" *piña* leaves and handwoven into an intricate, sheer fabric—is one of the oldest surviving indigenous arts of Antique and Aklan Provinces. The new Philippine silk called Neilino Silk appeared in the '90s from a collaboration between Filipina Jeanne Goulbourn and Korean Eun Il Lee. Their sericulture company now produces unique silk-blends that make tactile and sheer draperies for beds and windows. Natural ecru silk threads are combined with exotic metallic threads, or are married with *abaca*-hemp to make wall coverings.

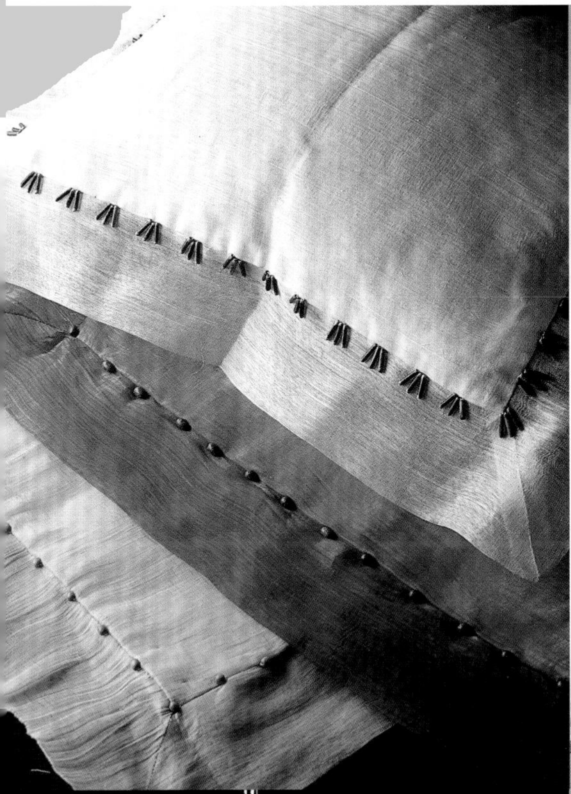

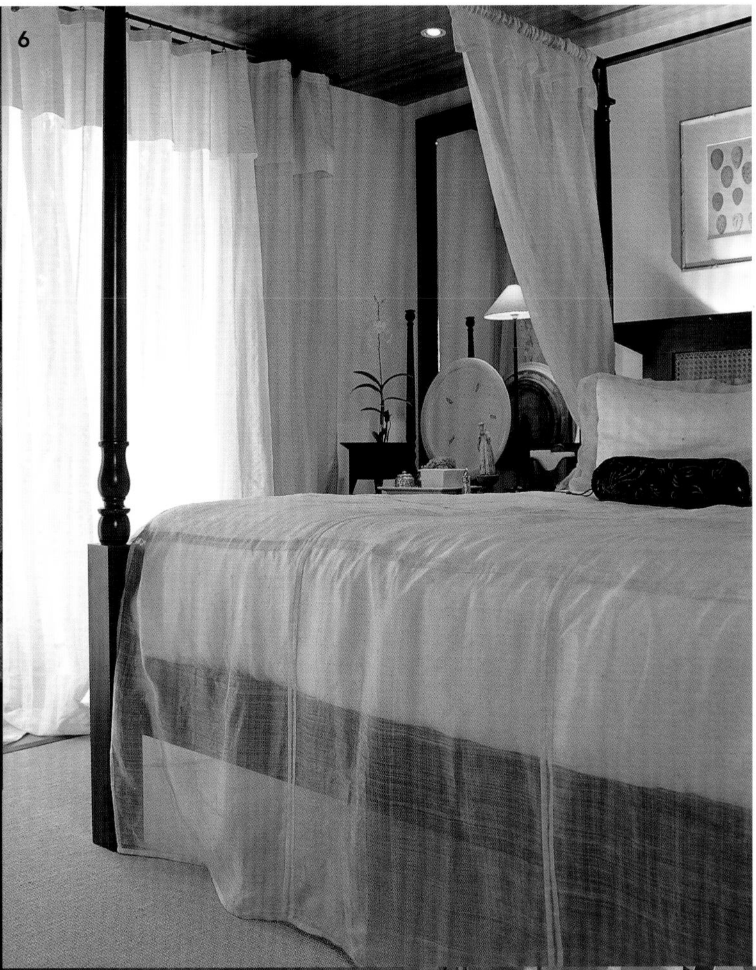
6

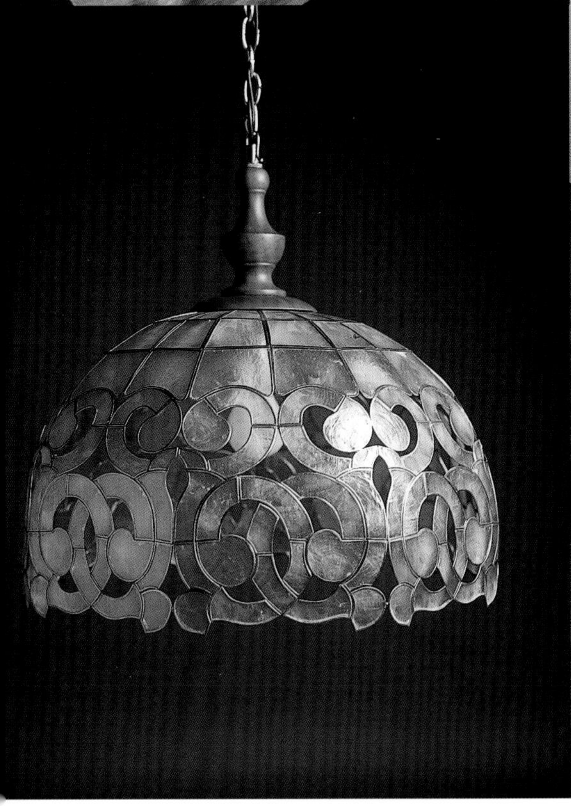

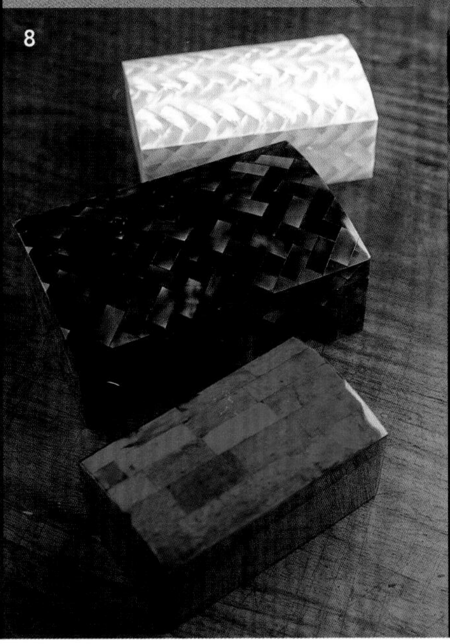
8

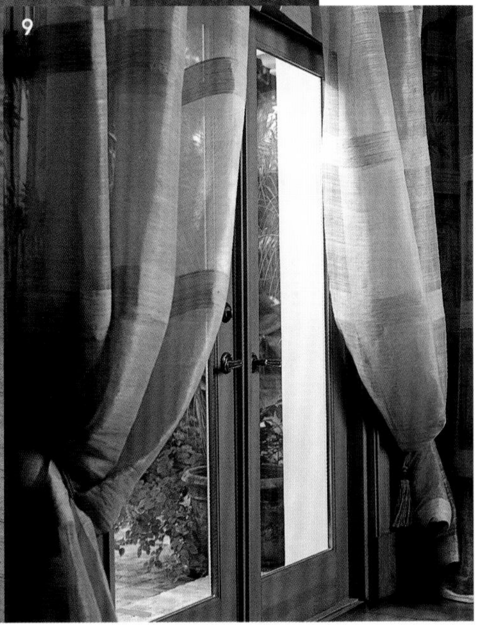
9

# ceramics

**1** Cream and sugar set with natural twig handles by Ugu Bigyan of Tiaong. Courtesy: Chelo Hofilena. **2** Multicolored stoneware plates by Lanelle Abueva. Woven and dyed *buntal* placemats by Elisa Reyes. **3** Mottled stoneware bowls with greenish glaze by Manolo Glema of Cagayan de Oro. **4** Celadon-glazed fluted bowl with Pinatubo ash-glaze by Lanelle Abueva of Antipolo. **5** Scarlet-glazed bowls with a blue comet by Jon Pettyjohn. Courtesy: Yola Perez. **6** Long tall earthy flower vase by Tessy Pettyjohn of Pansol. **7** Slip-molded coffeepots by Lanelle Abueva of Antipolo. **8** Three-piece brown eyrie candle-holder by Tessy Pettyjohn. **9** Holey stoneware bowl by Manolo Glema of Cagayan. **10** Fingerprinted stoneware bowl by Jaime de Guzman of Candelaria.

Earth materials, such as clay and stone, resonate with the qualities of nature and bring the outdoors into the home. The tactile art of studio pottery emerged in Manila in the mid-'70s, in the earthy works of Jaime and Anne de Guzman. Their rustic clay pots were created from natural materials sourced from Laguna to Sagada. Lately Jaime is producing stoneware that is transformed into percussion drums. In the '80s, Fil-American Jon Pettyjohn found in Pansol, Laguna, a fertile ground to cultivate his own fine, Japanese-trained art of ceramics. Jon and his wife Tessy now run a pottery workshop where they teach clay-craft methods and turn out their own exquisite lines of art-ceramics—with Japanese airs. Lanelle Abueva Fernando, a potter based in Antipolo, east of Metro Manila, produces a wide range of molded stoneware and glazed ceramics that make their way into eclectic homes and restaurants. Ugu Bigyan is a potter, vine-weaver, and natural craftsman based in Tiaong, Quezon. He designs whimsical notions in clay, the most organic creations of all.

# coconut crafts

**1** Cocoshell-veneered table—three round tiers of a coco-veneered occasional table bear two glazed stoneware jars by Jon Pettyjohn. Table-design: Budji Layug. **2** Cocoshell noodle bowl: half a coco-shell makes a picturesque vessel for rice-noodles. Courtesy: Chelo Hofilena. **3** "Silapeng" wooden eggs—the lightweight *lipang* wood of the Cordillera is brushed and burnt (to display its cedar-like grain) and displayed in a reproduction of an Ifugao ritual bowl. Design: Silahis Crafts, Manila. **4** Cocoshell candlestick group—two tall coco-disk towers are mod candleholders; designed by Reimon Gutierrez. Turned wood-cylinder candleholders of varied heights; designed by Marcelo Alonzo. Pregnant queen piece from all-wood chess set; designed by Benjie Reyes. Courtesy: Firma. Photo by Felix Guinto. **5** Oriental gift boxes—ornamental wooden boxes trimmed with rattan side-weaving and colored tassels. Design: Silahis Crafts, Manila. **6** Cocoshell candles—citronella-scented candles in the half-coconut shells keep the mosquitos away. Design: Silahis Crafts, Manila. **7** Coco-woven jewelry box—coconut-shell cut and arrayed in basket-weave veneer on jewelry box. **8** Cocowood table—small square cocowood table frame is topped with round white Romblon marble top. Design: Silahis Crafts, Manila. **9** *Narra* flatware—freeform handles of *narra* wood, the Philippines' national wood, make handsome dining utensils. Courtesy: Tesoro's, Makati.

The coconut palm is often called the "tree of life," as all its parts contribute to nurturing tropical life. Filipinos cherish the coconut for its fleshy white meat (from young *buco* to mature *niog*) , its tasty milk (*gata*), and its rich, distinctive cooking oil. They also harness the coconut's versatile building parts: The fibrous husk of the mature coconut fruit provides coir for matting; the hard coco-shell, cleaned and dried, becomes a vessel, a rice bowl, a candleholder, or a veneering material; the coco-palm leaves are stripped and woven into hats, mats, baskets, and temporary shelters; the palm ribs (*ting-ting*) become stick brooms and furnishing décor; and the dried coco-flowers and twigs are fashioned into placemats and accessories. Lately, it is the coconut trunk that has taken the spotlight—in hardy rural furniture. What was once a fibrous and dusty throw-away lumber is now carefully selected, tediously processed and hand-crafted into furniture by artisans at Silahis Handicrafts, a trader in native products.

3

4

5

6

7

8

9

# contemporary furniture

**1** "Tower-of-Kamagong" side table—four levels of two-toned solid *kamagong* wood can be rotated to alter the pattern. Design & courtesy: Ramon Antonio. **2** Sason armchairs—modern leather lines and rustic bamboo materials characterize twin black armchairs. Design: Bernie Sason of the Sason Shop, Bacolod. Courtesy: Lanelle Abueva Fernando. **3** Ellipse lounge chair—an extra wide leather armchair with mat-weave back and a stable, solid feel. Design: Val Padilla of Padua International. **4** Diamond-beveled cabinet—a classic wooden bar-cabinet from the furniture design center of Cebu. Design: Louisa de los Santos. Photo by Rene Araneta. **5** Shaker-inspired lounging chair and ottoman—a spare and modern adaptation in light maplewood. Courtesy: Designs Ligna. **6** "Linea" lamp—asymmetrical standing lamp in mahogany with rustic *abaca*-weave shade. Design: Val Padilla of Padua International. **7** Oriental minimal cabinet—a modern-classic collector's item in *narra* wood, trimmed with black *kamagong*. Design and courtesy: Ramon Antonio. **8** "Claire" fine leather-weave armchair—sleek lines characterize this best-seller chair. Design: Budji Layug.

Given wide exposure to the modern furniture of Europe and North America, Filipino designers have absorbed—and recreated—modernist designs for their private spaces. Architect Ramon Antonio collects Mario Botta and Philip Starck chairs and places them next to his classic Chinese *hong* wood armchairs. Then he designs one-of-a-kind contemporary furnishings celebrating Philippine hardwoods, wrought iron, and riverstone. The multi-talented Budji Layug has consistently fashioned fresh new home items using indigenous materials—from beaten bamboo and split rattan to fine-weave leather. He incorporates the natural veneers of dark or bleached coconut shell; upholsters refined armchairs with the fine white *sica* rattan from Palawan. New Filipino designers tend to focus on high-end furniture exports—after they are educated, exposed to world trends, and displayed in the annual furniture fairs of Manila and Cebu. Native adeptness and innate creativity with local materials is their forte: they can weave, laminate, inlay or mold a wide range of materials. Among the names to watch: Val Padilla of Padua International; Louisa de los Santos of Casa Cana in Cebu; and Bernie Sason of Sason Shop in Bacolod. They are making pieces which blend comfort with style and aesthetics with luxury, in designs that are local and original. Sason for one celebrates bamboo "for its warm, Oriental character." He combines Philippine wood and bamboo, steel and leather, to produce distinctive furniture.

# rustic-eclectic collections

**1** *Escritoryo*—cane and wood panels in a modern writing desk. Design: Designs Ligna. **2** Three-seater bench—loveseat for three (the chaperone sits in between). Courtesy: Claude Tayag. **3** *Tocador*—chest of drawers with beaten-bamboo panelling. Design: Designs Ligna. **4** *Papag*—traditional cane weave day-bed on simple carved posts, in Ilocos style. Courtesy: Claude Tayag. **5** *Kabayo* head—wooden detail of a horse or pig. Courtesy: Claude Tayag. **6** *Calado* wood panels—carved and cutout architectural details from a traditional Filipino house. **7** Japanese-style refectory table (under diptych by Arturo Luz) and cross-legged ottoman seat below. Courtesy: Budji Layug. **8** *Mesa altar*—traditional altar table has bone inlay ornamentation. Reproduction: Tawalisi, Makati. Courtesy: Manny Minana. **9** *Kambal aparador*—custom-made closet. Design by Omeng of Osmundo's. Courtesy: Catherine Zobel. **10** Ifugao *aparador*—heavy cabinet from the Cordillera made of hardwood, fastened by tongue and groove method without nails. Courtesy: Claude Tayag. **11** *Butaka*—planter's chair of *kamagong* wood and open-cane-weaving. Reproduction by Tawalisi. Courtesy: Manny Minana. **12** Shaker-style *aparador*—original 1920s cabinet. Courtesy: Yola Perez Johnson. **13** *Silya*—wooden loveseat in wood and open-cane weave. The large mural behind is minutely inlaid in fine-cut coconut shell. Courtesy: Chelo Hofilena.

Traditional Philippine furniture evolved in the late19th century from models that originated in rural homesteads; or were adapted from ornate church furniture, or were learned from Chinese craftsmen. Today, homeowners who treasure Filipino heirloom furniture find few items at antique shops in Manila, so more often settle for handsome reproductions or restorations. Reputable dealers and connoisseurs—Osmundo's, Tawalisi, Via Antica, Baylosis and Hidalgo's—have moved into restoration, adaptation, and reproduction of traditional furniture, their new renditions looking just like the ancestral item. For rustic heirloom designs, Omeng Esguerra of Osmundo's is Manila's finest craftsman with natural-hewn hardwoods. In a more modern-classic mode, Designs Ligna has lately been designing along modernized Philippine-inspired lines. Design Ligna products are now lightened, softened and updated by designer Dem Bitantes, an avowed minimalist. He says of his own clean, straightforward lines: "If you design for less, you design for more."

# handwoven fabrics

**1** Tribal weaves of Northern Luzon—Ilocos *abel* weaves from La Union and optical *binacol* weaves from Vigan. Collection: Elizabeth Reyes. **2** Modern *t'nalak* weaving—handloomed *abaca* fabrics, woven by T'boli tribespeople of Cotabato. Design and courtesy: Galerie Dominique. **3** Northern tribal weavings—traditional fabrics of the Tingguians of Abra; and the Ifugaos of Bontoc. Collection: Claude Tayag. **4** Patadjong—traditional cotton plaid fabric for the tube-skirt, worn by rural Tagalogs and Visayan women. Collection: Elizabeth Reyes. **5** Yakan weaves of Sulu—both traditional and modern geometric weaves of the Yakan tribespeople of Basilan, Sulu. Collection: Elizabeth Reyes. **6** Bark-cloth hanging—two wild natural fibers are stripped, retted, and woven into a long hanging panel. Courtesy: Silahis Crafts. **7** Banana-rayon covers—fine *abaca* banana fiber mixed with rayon and dyed flourescent colors for throw pillows. Design: Narda's Ikat.

The Philippines harbors a great number of minority ethnic tribes, primarily in the mountain regions of north and south. Each group produces distinctive home-grown, naturally dyed cotton or hemp weavings using the traditional backstrap loom—an unwieldy, multi-stranded affair stretched between a woman's hip and a high post. Diverse ethnic cloths of the Cordillera are highly prized—Ifugao tribal weaves are restrained and ritualistic; Bontoc are bold and colorful; and Kalinga weaves the most decorative with bits of shell and bone. Sagada-born Narda Capuyan has creatively developed and marketed a contemporary *ikat* since the '70s. Narda spins the traditional *ikat* of her community into modern-day tapestries, throw-pillows and household linens—weavings that have found their way to Bloomingdale's, New York. The Ilocos Region—starting from La Union and up to Abra—has seen a revival and appreciation of handloom weaving in recent years. The geometric ceremonial blankets of the Itneg or Tingguian tribe have emerged as the remarkable, collectible fabrics of the highlands, while *abel*, the traditional weave of Ilocos blankets, has been redeveloped recently for clothing material. The indigo-colored optical *binacol* fabric of Vigan has been adapted as ethnic upholstery. Handweaves from the Muslim tribes of Mindanao are exotic collectibles in imported silks and cottons; as well as proud assertions of cultural individualism. The five main groups of the south—Maranao, Maguindanao, Tausog, Yakan, and Samal—share a color sensibility for red-violets, blues, rich ochres and magentas. It is the Yakan tribe who weave the most intricate and decorative fabrics that become ethnic table linens and tapestries.

# organic lights

**1** Dining table centerpiece—nature's own hanging lamp made of bamboo twigs wrapped with translucent resin panes. Design: Wendy Regalado. **2** Banana cloth lamps—fine *abaca*-banana fiber mixed with rayon make natural-glow standing lamps. The shades are made of raffia from the *buri* palm; the rough-hewn bench is a *molave* master-piece. Design: Dita S Ong. **3** Resin and twig lamps—three small garden lanterns made from bamboo twigs and resin panels. Design: P J Aranador for Elm and Oak Inc, Bacolod. **4** Silk and sushi lamp—Thai silk shade over a sushi plate by Lanelle Abueva. Design: Chito Vijandre. Courtesy: Firma Shop. Photo: Felix Guinto. **5** Paper pulp vases—white bowls and flower vases made from laminated paper pulp. Design: Tony Gonzales of Greeting Card Company. **6** Four-leaf lamp—two-foot tall lamps of resin panes around metal frame. Design: Reena G Pena. Courtesy: Firma Shop. Photo: Felix Guinto. **7** Nature's way accent lamp—hanging lamp made from a grid of bamboo twigs and resin panes. Design: Wendy Regalado. **8** Cylinder table lamp—rustic handmade paper wrapped round a bamboo frame. Design: Wendy Regalado. **9** Shell wall lamp—over 100 white cockle shells are wired together and lit from behind. A best-seller art-light, designed by Milo Naval of Evolve. Photo by Felix Guinto. **10** Etched *capiz* lamp—*capiz*-shell dust is etched in modern square panes onto this glass-jar candle-holder. Design: Carlo Tanseco of Kaizenhaus. Courtesy: Firma Shop. **11** Ostrich egg lamp—wood base from Bangkok; ostrich egg shells from Davao. Design: Chito Vijandre. Courtesy: Firma Shop. Photo: Felix Guinto.

In the field of home accessories Filipinos demonstrate their innate creativity with materials—of both the natural and non-traditional kind. Native inventiveness wields a special spirit upon coco-shells and sea shells; on handmade paper, pulp, and wires, on translucent resins and tree twigs. Among the names to watch for modern designs in household wares: Carlo Tanseco—a young product designer who gives familiar items a novel twist or a stylish nuance that takes its basic function to a fresh aesthetic level. His ceramic jars, vases, trays, baskets, and iron-and-weave furniture—all have a rustic-contemporary appeal for the new-generation. Prolific designer Milo Naval has a geometric and modern eye for organic materials. He makes a wall-lamp of a hundred shells wired together. Tony Gonzales sculpts contemporary household items with common paper pulp. Architect Wendy Regalado makes naturalist-intuitive lamps of parchment and resin, stretched over twigs from her backyard bamboo bush. Designer Chito Vijandre, owner of Malate's outre gift shop Firma, orchestrates silk and ceramic, fashion sense, and ostrich eggs to make unique lamps, vases and conversation pieces.

# marble & stone

**1** Sound of Nature"water fountain—water trickles over natural stones. Design: Michelle Kearney. Courtesy: Firma. **2** Marble fruits—white Romblon marble carved into cool hard tropical sculptures. Courtesy: Soumak, Manila. **3** Inner light lamp— the golden marble of Romblon forms the lamp-base under rough *abaca* shade. Design: Soumak, Manila. **4** The dish, the clock and the tealight—accessories made from the striated black serpentinite stone. Design: Zambrox. **5** Bookends and accents— accessories made of sandy volcanic-rock. Design: Silahis Crafts, Manila. **6** Lava-Rock *bulols*—rice god figures made of lava-rock, as candleholders. Design: Silahis Crafts, Manila. **7** Black marble bookends—modular bookends frame a CD or book library. Design: Mark Gillen of CarvedMarble.com, Angeles. **8** Stone table—square occasional table veneered in white Mactan marble fossil stone. Design: Leo Yao of Diretso. **9** Stoneware bowls— handcarved stone bowls in sandstone, gray and black serpentinite. Design: Zambrox, Manila. **10** Stony lights—carved stone lamp-base on a giant table-slab of black serpentinite; and two "flintstone" tealight holders. Design: Zambrox, Manila. Photos 1,4,9,10 by Felix Guinto.

Marble, stone, and clay are materials that bring the textures and colors of nature inside the home. The beauty and tactility of stone satisfies a primal need to be connected with the earth. Artist-marble-carver Mark Gillen sculpts in Romblon marble—after creating marble items for the Museum of Modern Art in New York for over ten years. "It's a unique challenge working stone," he says, "it's the most tangible material—tactile, sensual, with veins of colour, and even smell." Gillen has produced fountains, tables, bookcases, and bathtubs in this cool elegant material. Aficionados acknowledge the translucent white marble with beige or purple or light greenish veins of Mindoro and Romblon Islands as the true hard marble stone of the islands. Except for rare commissioned works, marble-carving today is relegated to production of ashtrays, bowls and lamp bases. Lately these light marbles have been joined by the black serpentinite stone and beige sandstone from the mountain ranges of Zambales Province. Zambrox, a family company, produces small fossil-stone accessories in rocks with light grayish-green to greenish-black hues.

# modern mixed-media

**1** Yin and Yang armchairs—the metal and wicker structure is hand-wrapped in rattan splits, leaving a voluminous, yet light chair. Design: Betty and Kenneth of Interior Crafts of the Islands, Cebu.
**2** Balou armchair—a light, strong, airy exercise in structure and form, utilizing wicker, metal, and *abaca* rope. Balou was voted "Designers' Choice by *World of Interiors Magazine.* Design: Kenneth Cobonpue of Interior Crafts, Cebu. **3** Serpentina armchair and footrest—sinuous chair frame of wrought iron with *abaca*-hemp woven seats; and matching centipede ottoman. Design: JLQ International, Cebu. Photo by Rene Araneta.
**4** Virgo chaise lounge—modernist loveseat in bleached banana-trunk fibers woven on a metal frame. Best Design Awardee 2000: Leo Yao of Diretso. **5** Winged armchair—giant modular furniture piece composed of dyed *abaca* rope shaped and woven over wooden frame. Extended side-wing arms can hold book and coffee. Design: Milo Naval of Evolve Designs. **6** PJ bamboo lamps—standing lamps of turned bamboo columns and criss-crossed bamboo twigs, with handmade paper shade with crushed bamboo leaves. Design: PJ Aranador for Iloilo Super Art Furnishings of Iloilo. **7** LC metal chair—modern space-age design using aluminum-finished metal and Girard fabric covers. Design: Lor Calma Designs. **8** LC Solihiya—modular chair and footstool comprising bamboo legs and fine durable cane weave seats. Design: Lor Calma Designs. **9** Linea armchair—'50s-style inspired best-seller chair of dyed open-weave structure made of rattan-split and stainless steel. Design: Kenneth Cobonpue of Interior Crafts of the Islands, Cebu. **10** *Abaca* table—low square coffeetable of plaited *abaca* rope moulded round a glass top. Design: Milo Naval of Evolve Designs. **11** Lampa loveseat—sofa of woven *lampakanai* rope and leather strips; iron legs with antiqued silver finish. Design: Murillo's, Cebu. Photo by Rene Araneta. **12** LC wicker-S chair—large serpentine metal frame is woven with rattan wicker-weave seating. Design: Lor Calma Designs.

Organic materials treated with modern technology give rise to eclectic modern furnishing. *Abaca*-hemp is plaited and molded to wood, or wrapped around wrought iron; wicker-rattan takes on a sinuous grace clinging to metal. Bamboo is turned, smoothed, melded with aluminum. The strongest design trend in recent years is the use all-natural rustic materials. International architect Lor Calma makes quiet waves with his singular furniture pieces: serpentine or linear LC chairs demonstrate his refined and modernist taste, using cane-wicker joined finely with brushed metal or compressed bamboo framework. Ken Cobonpue of Interior Crafts of the Islands has originated three *abaca*-wrapped "transparent" armchairs—unique exercises in positive and negative spaces and volumes that are catching attention and orders abroad. Other abstract concepts and interesting notions are born from this Pratt-educated designer who leans toward stark modernity and favors "the elimination of everything that is not essential." Milo Naval of Evolve Designs elevates commonplace organic materials with his instinctively modern and graphic sensibility. Constantly inspired by everyday natural materials, Milo expresses tactile messages with plaited, molded hemp, woven vines, and varnished bamboo; and produces thoroughly modern furnishings with a naturalist's ease. Leo Yao of Diretso works with a range of mixed media from Mactan's fossil stone to bleached banana trunk—to produce eye-catching, collector's item furnishings.

3

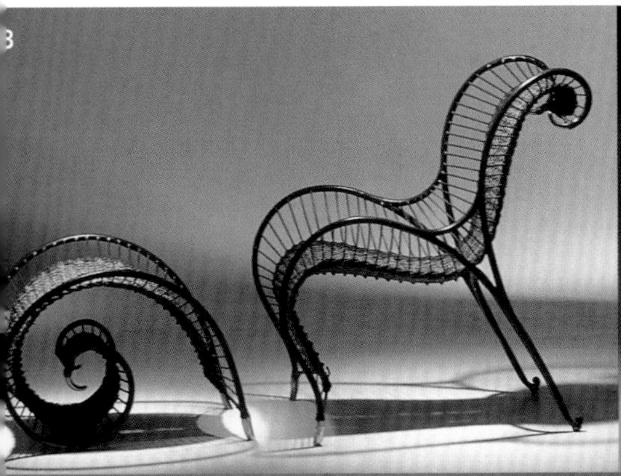

4

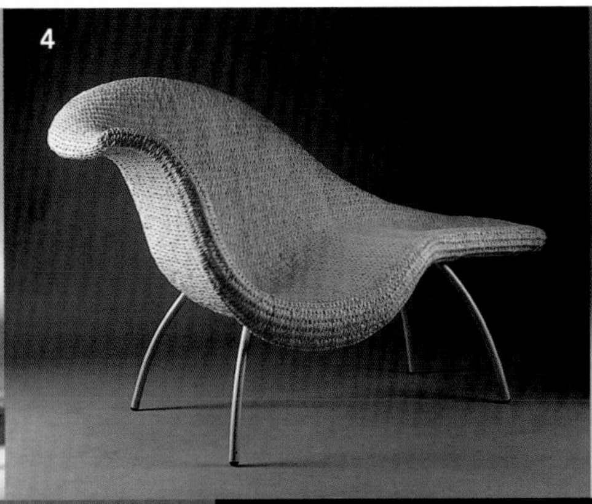

5

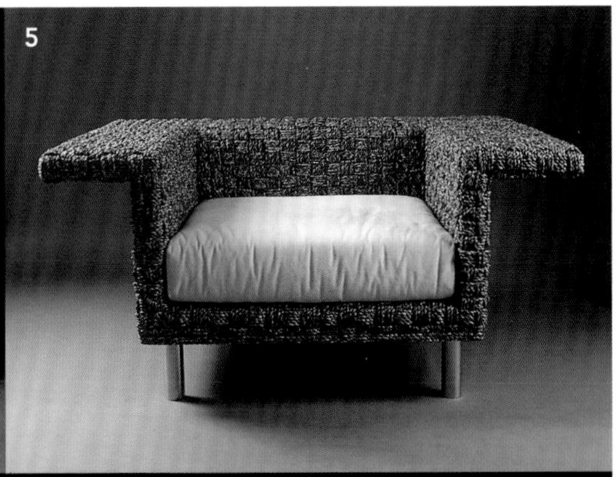

6

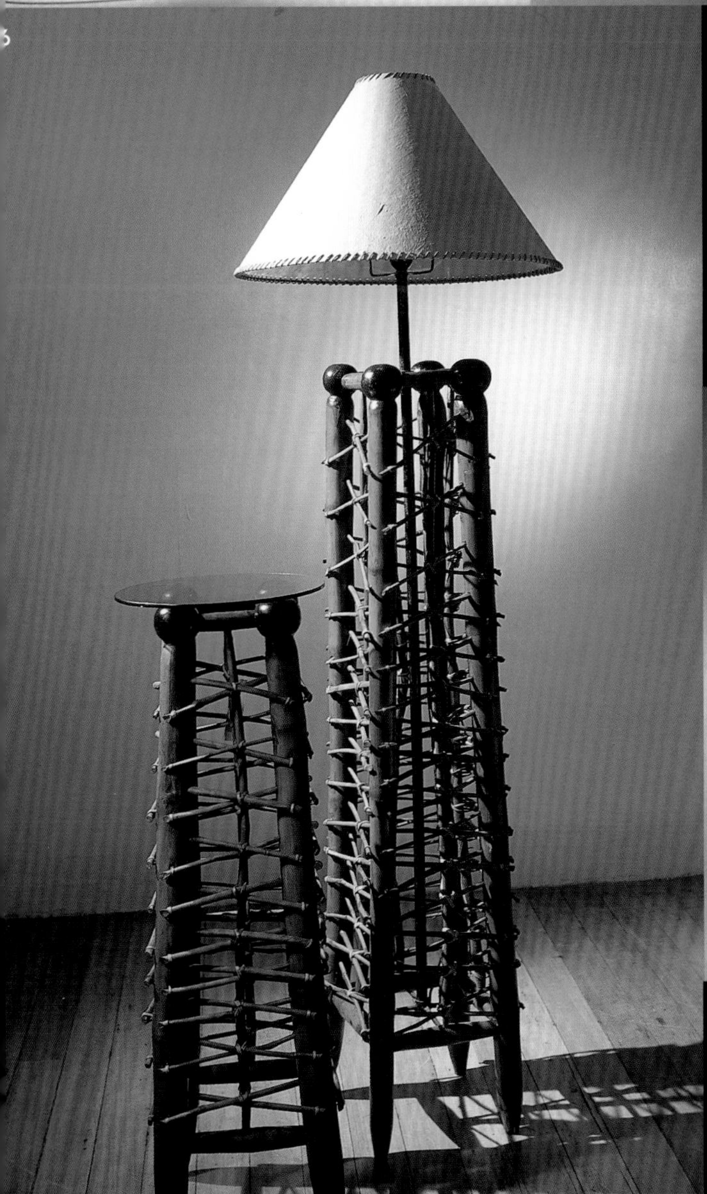

7

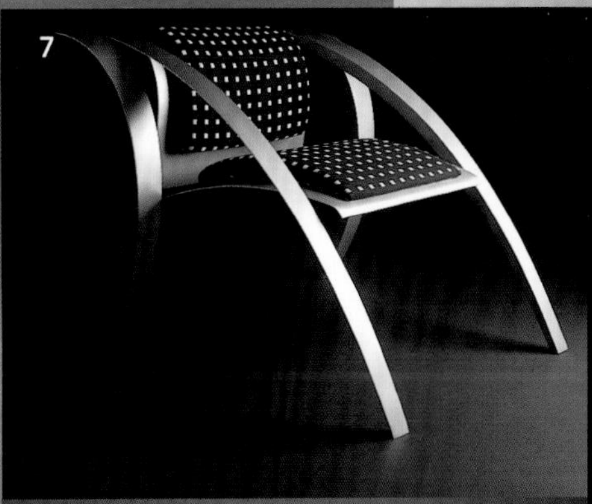

8

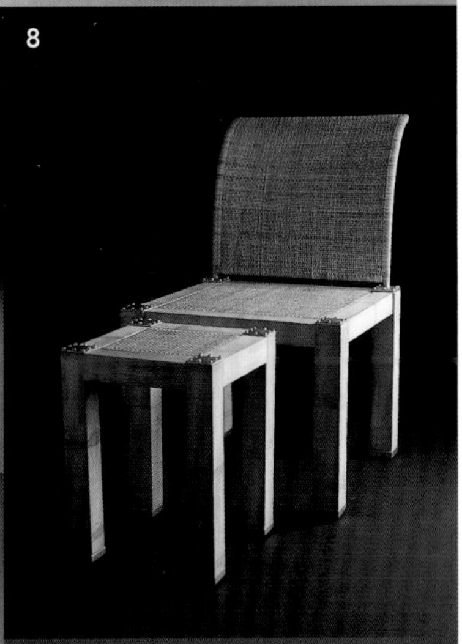

9

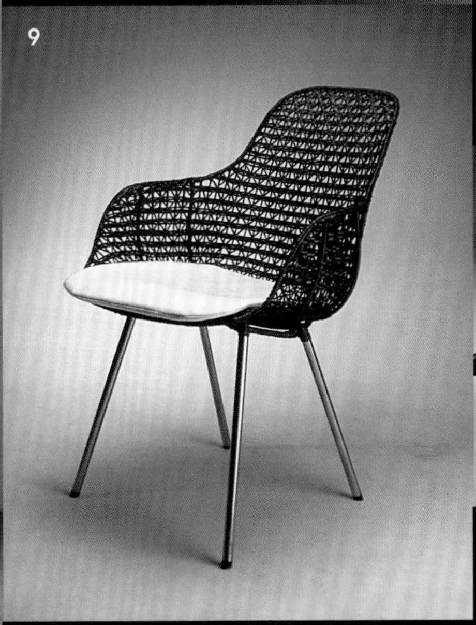

10

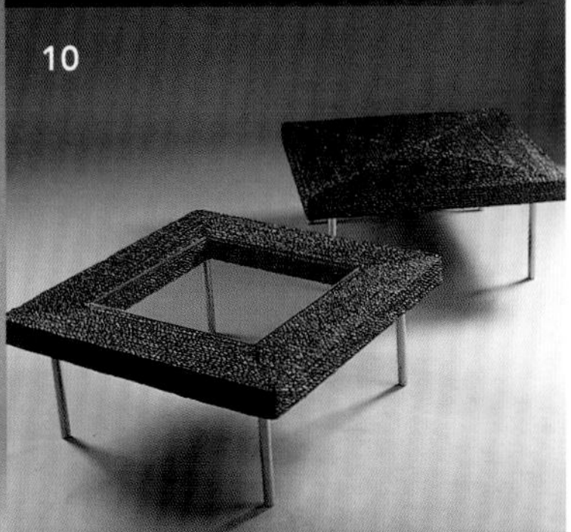

11

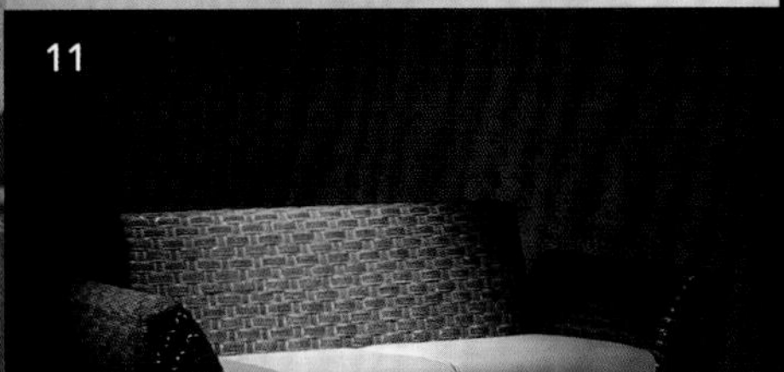

12

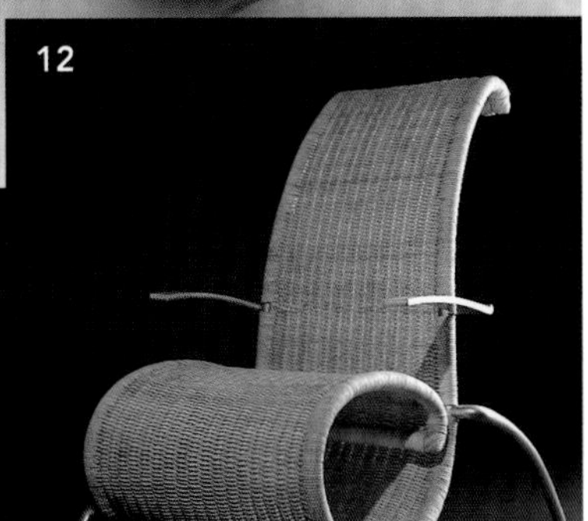

# rattan & cane

**1** Tuscany seat—oversized armchair covered with flattened rattan-weave over large, spiral-fluted arms. Design: Elmar Dammann for Castilex of Cebu. Courtesy: Sigi of Antipolo. **2** Crescent loveseat—semi-circular sofa with woven rattan splits over solid bamboo frame. Design: Design Ventures of Cebu. Photo by Rene Araneta. **3** Orientalia armchair—in rattan vines and fine bamboo sticks. Design: Obra Cebuana of Cebu. Photo by Rene Araneta. **4** Manhattan lounge chair—split rattan weave armchair with leather covered cushions. Design: Primafil, Manila. Courtesy: Lifestyles, Rockwell. **5** Madame X armchair—flamboyant armchair made of malleable permacane, a specialized rattan laminate (Bill Clinton has one). Design: Yrezabal Inc, Manila. **6** Lupo loveseat—whimsical sofa of fine leather weave, beaten-bamboo backrest; and rattan poles forming a loop under the arms. Design: Ramon Castellanos of Diseno en Asia, Cebu. **7** Malacca rocking chair—fine Malacca cane fashioned into a refined rocker. Design: E Murio, Manila. Courtesy: Lifestyles, Rockwell. **8** Cane and leather daybed—fine Malacca cane and fine leather-weave matting in a refined seat. Design: E Murio, Manila. Courtesy: Lifestyles, Rockwell. **9** Kelly lounge chair—woven rattan splits over a comfy horseshoe-shaped armchair. Design: Yrezabal, Manila.

There are some 600 species of rattan palms native to the rainforests of Southeast Asia, but only a handful of varieties remain for modern furnishing—younger, shorter, and thinner rattan vines. Manufacturers have had to import higher-grade raw materials from China and Vietnam. But Filipino designers have produced wondrous furnishings off the dwindling vine. The fascination starts with rattan's prime characteristic—its flexibility. Also, its many sizes and varieties: from the *yantoc*, a field rattan, to the pithy, dense *arurog*, to the new rattan *sica*, the young smooth and white rattan grown in Palawan. At the center of the industry are the rustic furnishings made by companies such as Primafil. In contrast there is the refined "Indochine appeal" of "Malacca" cane furnishings by Eduardo Murio: he uses almost exclusively a fine smooth cane imported from China, and designs finely scaled models that are appropriate for small spaces. From Cebu emerges Ramon Castellanos, who approaches design with whim and fantasy. His colorful, individualistic furniture in modern rattan, leather, and bamboo go out by the label Diseno en Asia. And finally, there are pieces by Eduardo Yrezabal, owner and originator of the latest modern material permacane, a rattan laminate.

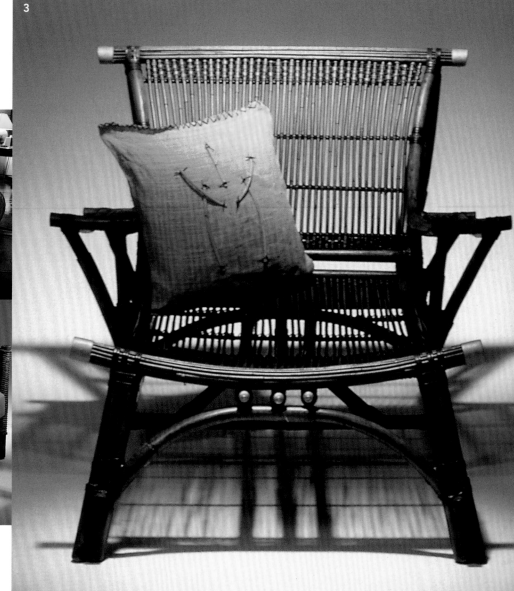

# wood art

**1** Rock-heavy table—rustic outdoor table is solidly weighed down by stone cylinders on trestles. Design: Ernest Santiago. **2** Two-ply TV-lounger—long chaise-lounge made of permacane frame with Abra-blanket cushion cover. Design: Claude Tayag; produced by Yrezabal Inc. **3** *Mesa altar* and a wavy *kamagong* wall-relief—modernized altar table is made of streaky *supa* wood. The wall sculpture comprises wavy pieces of black and brown *kamagong* wood. Design: Claude Tayag. **4** Elemental riverbed sofa—named because materials were found in Laguna rivers; gray java-rocks and a giant curved driftwood embrace the main *narra* plank. Design: Ernest Santiago. **5** Dancing to Rumors—wood screen divider of solid laminated *narra* (wood is precut in undulating shapes, joined and planed together). Design: Claude Tayag. **6** Reflections on wood and stone—river stones, straight-edged or natural, replace seat cushions and table tops. All furnishings by Ernest Santiago. **7** Stone throne—large black java-stone from the river is cradled by a modern metal frame. Design: Ernest Santiago. **8** Strange bedfellows coffeetable—sculptured table made of solid *molave*, with multiple finger-trunks. Design: Claude Tayag. **9** Grandfather armchair—modern take-off on the traditional rural armchair, with river-stone finials. Design: Ernest Santiago. **10** Wavy bench with four backrests—four-seater modernist bench recycled from one old post of red *balayong* wood. Design: Claude Tayag. **11** Benji horseshoe chair—three different types of local hardwood—*narra*, *kamagong* and *ipil*—are recycled and recreated into a modern seat; all-wooden pegs and hand-polishing to satin-smooth finish. Design: Benji Reyes. **12** Cordi chair—a chair of *molave* planks, fitted by tongue in groove construction. Design: Ernest Santiago.

The secret of hand-crafted wood art furniture lies in nature's materials, whereby a profound respect for the original character of the materials allows the essence of the wood to shine through. This restrained aesthetic is the common ground and spirit that moves modern art-furniture designers Claude Tayag, Ernest Santiago, and Benji Reyes. Composing fluid and graceful lines on old or found woods, they create spare, uncluttered, or non-traditional works that entice the eye and invite the touch. Visual impact and sensory appeal are equal considerations, alongside the materiality of functional furniture.

Claude Tayag collects antique furniture and old hardwoods and recycles these into modern-day art-furniture. Lately his artistic creations are defined by singular wavy planes on benches and sinuous curves on lounging chairs. Ernest Santiago loves nature, Laguna Province, river stones, driftwood and minimalist furniture—he makes elemental, rustic statements combining river stone with wood and metal. Benji Reyes produces wooden armchairs that combine natural old *narra*, *molave*, *yakal*, *kamagong*, and *ipil* with art-deco airs.

# acknowledgments

The author would like to thank the following for their help during the production of this book:
Coordination Assistance: Esperanza Fricke, Wendy Maramba, Mia Quimpo, Ami Rufino Starnegg. Photography Assistants: Rene Basilio, Felix Guinto. Photo favors (equipment and additional slides): Mitch Amurao, Tom Epperson, Miguel Fabie, Zac Moran & Melo Mondia, Lolito "Perry" Peregrino, Chopper Pilot, Lita Puyat, Denise Weldon. Accommodations: Mr. & Mrs. Carlos Cruz, Susanna B. Ortigas, Emma Matias & Martin Branner, DonJaime & Bea Zobel. Patrons, advisors, stylists: Florante Aguila, Ivy & Cynthia Almario, Jescel Cañedo of Cebu Furniture Industries Foundation, Connie Castro, Peter Cho's Color Workshop, HongKong, Jojo Crisanto, Isabel Diaz, Doreen Fernandez, Yola Perez Johnson, Robert Lane, Jun Makapugay, Ino Manalo, Pilar B. Miranda, Linda Nakpil, Johnny Ramirez, Malou Antonio Veloso. Architect Interviewees: Pablo Antonio Jr, Ramon Antonio, Eduardo Calma, Lor Calma, Reimon Gutierrez, Andy Locsin, Francisco "Bobby" Mañosa, Manny Miñana, Ted Narciso, Conrad Onglao, Jose Pedro "Bong" Recio, Benji Reyes, Noel Saratan, Benny Velasco, Joey Yupangco. Additional Photography: Tom Epperson (pages 35, 202), Felix Guinto (pages 206, 214, 216, 217), Neil Lucenta & Claudine Sia (pages 114–118), Rene Araneta (pages 219, 220).